Pride of the Nation:
Dr. A.P.J. Abdul Kalam

Mahesh Sharma

DIAMOND BOOKS

©Publisher

Publisher : **Diamond Pocket Books (P) Ltd.**
X-30, Okhla Industrial Area, Phase-II
New Delhi-110020
Phone : 011-40712200
E-mail : sales@dpb.in
Website : www.diamondbook.in

Pride of the Nation: Dr. A.P.J. Abdul Kalam
By - *Mahesh Sharma*

Dr. Abdul Kalam was a true Indian and a great patriot. Truly secular, this first citizen of India had passionately studied Bhagwad Gita along with Quran Sharif and imbibed the teachings of these great Holy Scriptures in his life. He was a vegetarian and a teetotaler who believed in the doctrine of non-violence and life based on values.

Publisher's Note

"Dream is not that which you see while sleeping it is something that does not let you sleep."

–Dr. A.P.J. Abdul Kalam

"Whatever may be the depth of water in a river, lake or pond; whatever may be the condition of water—cold, warm or stormy—the lotus will always surface and bloom."

These lines of saint poet Thiruvalluvar befit former President of India, Dr. Abul Pakir Jainulabaddin Abdul Kalam. He reached the highest post in spite of difficulties and struggles in life which people can ever imagine. This is the reason why he always people to see dreams. Our dreams appear before us in the form of ideas. We strive hard to turn ideas in reality.

A man must achieve his objective with firmness and conviction even if it appears to be impossible. All of us know that success does not come easily. We face lots of hurdles but we surrender to them. Rather we must win over them with wisdom and courage. With these ideals, Dr. Kalam reached the coveted Presidential Palace starting from a small cottage of Dhanushkodi (Rameshwaram).

President Dr. Kalam said that human brain is an unparalleled gift. You can travel through it. You should have inquisitiveness and studiousness.It is full of miracles of the universe.

He suggested that the thoughts should be transformed into assets. He said that life was full of ups and downs but success came only to those who conquered hardships. In his opinion—

1. Thoughtfulness is the source of progressiveness.

2. Thoughtless people bring stagnation to the Organisations and to the country also.

3. Thoughtfulness is the source of inspiration for action.

4. Without action, knowledge becomes useless and irrelevant.

5. Knowledge with action changes misfortune into fortune.

President Kalam liked to ask questions. He also loved to talk children. In his lifetime,he had met more than 3 lac children. He could see the future of India in the eyes of these children.

He hoped for a developed nation from children.

He dreamt of a vision of India that it would be a highly developed nation of the world by the year 2020. We should make whole-hearted efforts to fulfil his desires and dreams.

He had enormous faith in children and youth to transform his dreams into reality. Dr. Kalam dreamt of flying an aircraft in his childhood. He turned his dreams into reality. He soared high along with his country. "Prithvi", "Akash", "Trishul", "Naag" and "Agni", were his dreams and all of them came true. All these five dreams are the five elements which constitute every Indian. There is no doubt that Dr. A.P.J. Abdul Kalam will stand as a guideline for all the coming generations.

Dr. Kalam made India a self-dependent country in development of atomic power. All the human qualities like simplicity, agility, zeal and aspiration were present in him since his childhood. He lived with simplicity and yet he maintained the dignity of his position.

He was invited at a meeting in Delhi by the then Prime Minister Indira Gandhi when he successfully launched SLV- 3. He thought he looked shabby in his simple dress and sandals when he reached Delhi for the meeting . Prof. Satish Dhawan commented to encourage him, "Kalam, you are beautifully dressed with your successes."

A degree of doctorate is considered to be coveted and tough achievement for a man and yet Dr. Kalam was adorned with the degrees of "Doctor of Science" (D.Sc.) by 30 universities and teaching institutions. These degrees are symbolic of his great personality.

Dr. Kalam was a rare legend. It is very difficult to describe his greatness in words. The manifold aspects of a scientist, philosopher, great human being and a President are embodied in one person which is a source of inspiration for us.

– Narender Kumar Verma
nk@dpb.in

Contents

1. Dr. Kalam–Important Events of life

Full Name	:	Abul Pakir Jainulabaddin Abdul Kalam
Famous Name	:	A.P.J. Abdul Kalam
Great Grandfather's Name	:	Abul
Grandfather's Name	:	Pakir
Father's Name	:	Jainulabaddin
Mother's Name	:	Ashiyamma
Date of Birth	:	15th October, 1931
Birth Place	:	Dhanushkodi (Rameshwaram), Tamil Nadu
Primary School	:	Swartz High School,
	:	Ramanathapuram
1950	:	Admission in B.Sc. in St. Joseph College, Tiruchirapalli
1954-57	:	Passed degree course from Madras Institute of Technology (M.I.T.)
1958	:	Appointed as Senior Scientific Assistant in D.T.D.P. (Aeronautics)

1962	:	Decision of establishing Equatorial Rocket Launching Station (T.E.R.L.S.) in Thumba.
21st November, 1963	:	Successful launching of India's first sounding Rocket 'Nike Apache' from Equatorial Rocket Launching Station of Thumba.
20th November, 1967	:	Take off of Rohini Rocket from Equatorial Rocket Launching Station of Thumba.
1968	:	Formation of Indian Rocket Society. Thumba Equatorial Rocket Launching Station was dedicated to United Nations Organisation.
8th October, 1972	:	Successful testing of RATO (Rocket Assisted Take Off System) Successful flight-testing of SUKOI-16 jet aircraft by the country-made ERATO.
1976	:	Sad demise of his father at the age of 102 years and that of his mother after a short interval.
18th July, 1980	:	2nd operational launching of SLV 3. Successful establishment of Rohini Satellite in the orbit.
31st May, 1981	:	The first improvised launching of SLV-3. The establishment of R.S-D1 Satellite in the orbit. Successful launching of APIL (19th June 1981), Bhaskar-II (20th November 1981).

February, 1982	:	Appointmed as Director, D.R.D.L.
27th July, 1983	:	Launching of I.G.H.D.R
26th June, 1984	:	The first testing of Devil Missile.
3rd August, 1985	:	Foundation of the building of Research Centre.
September, 1986	:	Flight-testing of Prithvi Missile.
22nd May, 1989	:	Flight-testing of Agni Missile.
1990	:	Honorary degree of Doctor of Science (D.Sc.) by Jadavpur University.
1991	:	The degree of Doctor of Science (D.Sc.) by I.R.T. Mumbai.
July, 1992 to Dec. 1999	:	Scientific Adviser to Defence Minister.
1999 to 2001	:	Chief Scientific Adviser to the Government of India.
18th July, 2002	:	Elected as President of India.
25th July, 2002	:	ToTook oath as President of India.
Important Awards	:	B. Bharat Ratna (1997), Padma Vibhushan (1990) and Padma Bhushan (1981).
Other Awards	:	National Nehru Award, Arya Bhatta Award, Dr. Viren Roy Space Award, National Design Award, G.M. Modi Award, Om Prakash Bhasin Award, Lifetime Contribution Award in Engineering, Vir Savarkar Award, Indira Gandhi Award of National Integration.
27th July 2015	:	Passed away in Shillong at the age of 83

Journey from humble
beginning to greatness

A man comes to earth as an insignificant creature and after a long struggle, establishes his identity in the society. During this process, he faces many types of good and bad experiences. With these experiences only when he engages himself in creative thoughts and actions, he can aspire to be great; otherwise he is bound to fail and grope in darkness. Those who have the capability to emerge successful in their constructive pursuits have their names inscribed in golden words in the annals of history.

Our ex- President, Dr. A. P.J. Abdul Kalam, was one of the greatest personalities in this context. He was full of generosity and he rendered selfless service to humanity. He was dutiful, self-reliant and generous. Dr. Abdul Kalam was impressed by Indian spirituality and philosophy. In addition to his scientific acumen to make India one of the most powerful countries of the world, he was also a great believer in religion and spiritualism.

Introduction to His Life

The life of Dr. Abdul Kalam was not of mere illusive aspirations but it had its roots in solid ground of laborious achievements and experiences. World famous scientist and ex- President of India , Abul Pakir Jainulabaddin Abdul Kalam was born in a simple house situated in Mosque lane of the village Dhanushkodi (Rameshwaram) in Tamil Nadu on 15th October 1931. Since his childhood, Dr. Kalam was brilliant and wise. His father Jainulabaddin was neither highly literate nor rich. He was a boatman. Dr. Kalam liked boating very much since his childhood. He always liked to sail his boat safely to its destination through the sharp current with tides. He was self-dependent and earned money by selling newspapers than to accept any monetary help from anybody during his adolescence.

Dr. Kalam was in generally aloof even while he was with other children. While performing namaz with his father, he uttered the words of Arabic language without knowing the meaning contained therein but Dr. Kalam was convinced that his feelings and thoughts expressed through the prayer must reach God .With this tremendous faith he offered his prayer.

In the vicinity of Dr. Kalam's house, some Hindu families also lived. They did not care for difference of caste, creed and religion. Possibly this is one of the main reasons that Abdul Kalam had deep faith in the spirituality and philosophy of Hinduism as well as Islamic religion. This was apparent in his personality.

Abdul Kalam had unbounded aspirations to rise to a great height since his childhood.Whenever he saw a flying aeroplane, he too wanted to rise high in the sky and he could hardly suppress his desire. Struggling to rise in his career, he also appeared in the test for pilots but he could not succeed. His adventurous and hard-working nature did not let him lose his heart and he devoted himself wholeheartedly in the field of research and invention.

"Failure is the pillar of success" was proved by the fact that India became one of the advanced countries in the world of missiles. Rated as the topmost scientists of the world with his brilliant intellectual capability, Dr. Kalam not only launched Naag, Agni, Prithvi, Akash and Trishul etc. but also brought glory to India by gaining India's entry into the list of most powerful nations of the world.

Possibly nobody on earth could have imagined that the world famed nuclear scientist and basically a scholar like Dr. Kalam would be elected as the President of the greatest republic of the world. Dr. Abdul Kalam was brought up in a poor rural family but with his patience, labour and strong will, he was recognised not only as a great scientist in the entire world level but also rose to the position as President of the country.

Special traits

Moral values, faith and personality mould the character of a man. The character of a person decides his action and behaviour and this asset is so valuable that it cannot be bought even with the entire wealth in the world.

Dr. Kalam possessed all these qualities. The combination qualities like faith, goodwill, firm belief, hard labour with morality and human value in a single man—Dr. Kalam was a rare gem indeed.

Dr. Abdul Kalam was a true nationalist and a great patriot. These virtues helped him to became the first citizen of India. Though he is a Muslim by religion, he is well versed with Bhagvat Geeta along with Quran Sharif. He is a pure a vegetarian because he does not like to kill any creature. He has firm faith in God. He believes that the different forms of God described in the different religions are basically one and the same in essence.

Once a student asked him as to who was the ideal character in his opinion. He answered sharply—"Vidur. The great thinker and intellectual giant, an important character of Mahabharat, was simply a son of a maidservant. The main objective of his life was to establish dignity of religion. This is why he was against the unjust policies of Dhritarashtra and Duryodhana even when he was a Minister in the kingdom of Hastinapur."

Basically Dr. Kalam was a proud Indian, interested in Philosophy, spiritualism and also a hard working Indian scientist. In spite of holding the highest post of the country he was not conscious of the high rank, he used to meet the small school boys and youths with great love and simplicity which were unique. He looked for the future of India in them.

After becoming the President of India he travelled to almost all parts of the country without any display of lavishness in course of his journey. In the Presidential house also he always tried to keep the expenses incurred y the nation to the barest minimum. Even as President when he used to meet the Government officials, he made them understand his point like a teacher, and talked to them for hours. People always wanted to meet him and hear him .

Reflections

Mahatma Gandhi said— "The mental make-up of a man is formed by thoughts. If a man thinks that he is not capable of doing anything, he will actually be incapable of doing anything. To the contrary if he thinks that he is capable of performing impossible acts, he can make them possible and whatever may be the amount of labour and hardship, he would emerge successful."

The above comment aptly holds good for Dr. Kalam. Despite lack of education among his family members, Dr. Kalam with his strong acquired the highest level of education.

Dr. Kalam was interested in learning. He had ardent desire and urge for it. He sought admission in a nearby primary school. He had strong determination desire to study further and he was admitted in Swartz High School at Ramanathapuram from where he successfully passed matriculation examination.

Those days professional education was not common. Higher education simply meant going to the college. He took admission in St. Joseph College in Tiruchirapalli. In his college days, he developed great interest in Physics and English literature. Though Dr. Kalam could not get high marks, he passed the examination successfully. During those days he deeply studied astronomy too. Dr. Kalam used to study without anybody's help. There was nobody to guide him. In those hard days, he had two acquaintances named Jalaluddin and Shamsuddin from whom he gathered practical knowledge.

Jalaluddin was a local contractor and he used to help Dr. Kalam's father in his work. His father used to make boats. Later Jalaluddin got married to Johra, the eldest sister of Dr. Kalam and this way Jalaluddin and Kalam's friendship changed into close relatives. Though Jalaluddin was elder to Kalam by 15 years , they ware very close. Jalaluddin was the only man in the village of Kalam who knew how to read and write English. He always used to tell Kalam about scientific discoveries and inventions, literature and other interesting informations. He always encouraged Kalam to study further.

His other friend was his cousin Shamsuddin. He had a newspaper selling business at Rameshwaram. He used to run that agency all by himself. Later he engaged Kalam to assist him in the business.

It has been said that God helps those who help themselves. The association with these two friends proved to be a blessing for Kalam . One way Jalaluddin was a guide for his bright future. On the other hand Shamsuddin helped him to ease his financial constraint by paying salary for assisting him in his business. And provided an opportunity to Kalam to read almost all newspapers free of cost.

Dr. Kalam had no knowledge of any other alternative to higher education.He had admitted himself for the degree of bachelor of Science. He had a dream to fly high in the sky. After B.Sc., he felt that Physics was not very interesting —rather Engineering was better. So, he decided to take admission in M.I.T., but he required one thousand rupees to get admission and his father could not afford the fees. Under such circumstances his elder sister Johra came to his rescue and she arranged for the funds after mortgaging her ornaments including her chain and bangles. Dr. Kalam has mentioned in his autobiography that Johra had an ardent desire to see him highly educated. He was determined to stand first in M.I.T. examination and would return the mortgaged ornaments by repaying off the amount by his own earning.

There were two aeroplanes kept for display in the institute to help students to understand its technical functions. He was fascinated by those aeroplanes. He used to sit near those aeroplanes for hours and used to dream of flying them.

After completion of one year, he had to choose one specific subject. He opted for aeronautics. The only aim before him was to be a pilot.

His extreme politeness bordering on shyness and peaceful nature would hesitate him in asking for anything from anybody. This trait in his personality made him face a lot of hardships and obstacles. Sometimes he felt dejected and frustrated. But the inspiring words of his father encouraged him to win over his difficulties. His father always said, "One who can understand himself is the real wise man. Knowledge without wisdom is useless."

After getting his degree in aeronautics, he went to Hindustan Aeronautics Limited located in Bangalore for practical training. He learnt engine repairing and fitment of parts. He studied about the wings fitted in the super engine in great depth. Whatever he studied in the classroom helped him in understanding the practical aspect. He would study about the engine for hours. He also engaged himself in repairing work. During that period he wrote an essay in a Tamil journal with the heading "Let us build our own aeroplane". He received awards and gained popularity for this essay.

He had difficulties in getting a job after finishing the diploma course in aeronautical engineering. In those days, good opportunities were available in foreign countries which were far better than available in our country. Dr. Kalam had neither money nor the desire of going to a foreign land. Service to the nation was the only objective before him.

He applied to two institutions of Government of India for this purpose—firstly Air Force at Dehradun and secondly Defence Ministry in Delhi. For the first time in his life he went to Delhi from his native place Rameshwaram and appeared for the interview. After that he went to Dehradun for an interview. Only eight were to be selected out of twenty-five candidates. Air Force Selection Board used to put more emphasis on physical appearance rather than intelligence. He got 9th position in physical fitness so he was not selected.

When he failed to get a job of a pilot in the Air Force due to his physical weakness, he was in great despair when Swami Shivananda came to his rescue.

The saints of Rhishikesh filled his mind with new inspiration. Here he took bath in the Ganga river and walked towards Swargashram on a tour. He had read in his childhood that the saints can understand everything from their inner sense. In Swargashram he happened to meet Swami Shivananda, who looked like Buddha and Dr. Kalam was moved to see his glaring eyes and spiritually attractive face and he told him about his failure and despair.

On hearing Dr. Kalam, Swamiji looked into his eyes, as if he was preaching in silence.

After a pause, Swami Shivananda said— "Abdul Kalam, you reconcile and accept what is allotted to you and thus build up your career. The fate does not like you to be a pilot. The fate wants to make you something else. Universal consciousness, attracting latent energy and inner soul are related to God. Whatever He does, He does for the benefit of the human being. Go and search for some new goal." He gave him the spiritual preaching and pacified his disturbed mind.

After getting the spiritual inspiration from Shivananda's Ashram, Dr. Kalam set out on the way of progress after getting his blessings.

The preaching of Swami Shivananda taught him that a man can get joy by the grace of God. Joy and bliss are the two elements which are received by the creatures of earth. A man should ask from himself as to what is the role of the inner conscience in his life.

He went to the Department of Technology Development and Production (D.T.D.P.) to know the result of his interview.

Dr. Kalam was selected and in 1958, he was appointed as Senior Scientific Assistant on the monthly salary of Rs. 250/-. In Defence Ministry he was engaged in Technical Centre (Aviation). Kalam had developed confidence by thinking that if he could not fly an aeroplane, he could make the plane to fly. With this thought and confidence he headed towards the new direction wholeheartedly.

Here he was introduced to Sri R. Varadrajan who was in charge of the office. It was under his guidance that Dr. Kalam prepared the design

                    Pride of the Nation: Dr. A.P.J. Abdul Kalam

of Supersonic Fighter Plane. It was his first successful effort. Impressed with his achievement, the director of the institution Dr. Neelkanthan sent him to the unit of Aircraft and Armament Testing, Kanpur. In those days the testing of M.K.-1 aero plane was in progress on. Dr. Kalam played an important role in the execution of the procedures. After completion of the work at Kanpur Dr. Kalam came back to Delhi where he was told that he was included in the designing team for making the design of fighter-plane. 'DART. Young Dr. Kalam's happiness knew no bounds and he devoted himself wholeheartedly in the construction and development of its hot cockpit.

Time passed on. The Aeronautical Development Institute was established in Bangalore. Efficient and expert scientists were required to work there. Dr. Kalam was selected for the purpose. It was a challenging task for Dr. Kalam to work in the Aeronautical Development Institute, Bangalore because he had to establish a new record there. He decided to make a national hovercraft for which a team under his direction was constituted which included four engineers reporting to him. The period targeted to achieve success was 3 years.

It was not only a challenging task for Dr. Kalam but it was also full of obstacles. On the one hand none of the persons of the team had any experience and on the other hand there was great shortage of necessary spare-parts. Dr. Kalam had to face great hardships in the beginning but he was able to overcome the technical difficulties quite soon.

With all the knowledge he had gathered till that time and whatever resources were available, he decided to start the work. First of all he started preparing the design on a drawing board and engaged himself in preparing the hardware. Lastly with his hard work and devotion, he completed the light-weight and high-speed aeroplane without wings. The plane was named as 'Nandi'.

Dr. Kalam had proved that success actually meant achievement of the objective. But complete victory was yet to come.

After observing the achievements of Dr. Kalam, the then Defence Minister V.K. Krishna Menon reached Bangalore and expressed his desire to fly on the newly made plane. Dr. Kalam himself made the plane to fly successfully in the sky and landed it safely. This was the first victory in the form of success for Dr. Kalam.

After the completion and satisfactory launching of 'Nandi', Dr. Kalam surely looked forward to a great future. After the achievement of this success he wanted to make a more powerful hover-craft but unfortunately the Government of India stopped the programme.

Dr. Kalam was not disappointed. By then another important avenue opened before him. The Director of the Institute informed him that a very important guest -V.I.P. was coming to witness the demonstration of the hovercraft after a week.

Next week the guest reached there and expressed his desire to fly on that plane. It was a challenging moment for Dr. Kalam. He made the V.I.P. to perform the journey in the sky for 10 minutes. When the gentleman went back, Dr. Kalam came to know that the V.I.P. was none other than Prof. MGK Menon, Director of Tata Institute of Fundamental Research.

The following week, Dr. Kalam was invited for an interview in the Indian Committee for Space Research. The interview was for the post of Rocket Engineer. Dr. Kalam went to Bombay for the interview. Dr. Sarabhai and Prof. Menon took his interview. Dr. Sarabhai had a serious and earnest talk with him as if he was acquainted with him and his capability, Dr. Kalam was selected and he got an appointment letter which opened the doors for his further progress.

This achievement owed its success to the values he imbibed as a child –the values of dedication, hard work and commitment.

Childhood

Great thinkers proclaim that if a child is groomed to realise the importance of building character and thus learns to be responsible, half of the education is complete. This is true for Dr. Kalam.

Dr. Kalam was brought up in Tamil culture since his childhood and he was different than other boys of his age. He inherited sociability from his mother Ashiyamma. His father did not believe in material pleasures and hence Dr. Kalam also did not like to lead a life full of worldly pleasures and comforts. He would take his food in the kitchen itself. He liked to eat his sambar-rice on plantain-leaf. He relished the pickle and coconut-chutney served with the meal.

Abdul Kalam's childhood was full of struggles. Kalam would get up at 4 am, bathe, and then go for his mathematics class. His teacher would take only five students in the whole session; and bathing before class was a condition he had laid to all his students. After his morning class, Kalam along with his cousin Samsuddin went around town distributing the newspaper. As the town had no electricity, kerosene lamps were lit at his home between 7 pm and 9 pm. But because Kalam studied until 11, his mother would save some for him for later use. Mother Ashiamma was a simple religious woman. She played a huge role in shaping up Kalam's character and amazing personality. Being the youngest of seven brothers and sisters, Kalam was the dearest to his parents.

Kalam started going to a Primary School in his hometown Rameshwaram. Teachers were very impressed by Kalam's dedication towards study. One day, little Kalam could not attend school because of high fever. His class teacher Mr. Muthoot got worried. He headed straight to Kalam's house after school. The teacher also offered to help the family to treat Kalam and nurse him back to health soon.

Kalam's mother used to guide him through life's harsh realities. She taught him to judge goodness of life and differentiate it from all vices that may appear tempting. Her support served as soul soothing shade under scorching heat of life's hardships. She would serve him fresh breakfast as soon as he reached home after distributing newspapers. Kalam was a bright boy and passionate about his studies. His mother bought a small kerosene lamp for him so that darkness of night does not interrupt his studies. In one of his exclusive interviews, Kalam had mentioned all that his mother sacrificed for him. "Whatever I am today, it is because of my Mother," said Kalam.

Kalam's mother was very careful about his diet. Wheat is not widely available down the south. This is also the reason people living here follow rice as their staple food. However, Kalam was a fan of wheat chappatis. His mother made it a point that Kalam has at least two chappatis every day. Once, the family went short of wheat chappatis. Kalam's mother served him her own share of chappatis. When little Kalam got to know about this from his elder brother, he ran in tears and hugged the mother tight. His heart was filled with a unique sense of adoration and divine love for mother.

On the one hand he would visit the temple of Shiva every day which was at some distance from his house and on the other hand his father took him to an old mosque to offer Namaz (worship). His father was an ardent devotee of Allah. When his father came out of the mosque, people of different religions used to wait outside to greet him, many of them having bowl of water. His father used to dip the fingers in water and recite some Mantras, which then was given to the ailing to drink. People used to thank his father after they got cured. Seeing this, Kalam developed great faith in God since his childhood.

Ahmad Jalaluddin, who used to work with his father in making boats and later on became his brother-in-law, talked to him about spiritual matters and also about the power of God. Since childhood,

Dr. Kalam had firm belief that a person should not lose heart at the time of pain and sufferings, but he must face them boldly.

Dr. Kalam was attached to his mother and grandmother since childhood. She used to tell stories of the Ramayana and Prophet Mohammad. This is why Dr. Kalam had firm belief that there is some superpower which guides a man, shows the correct way and provides relief from the sufferings, difficulties and failures.

Like Mahatma Gandhi, Dr. Kalam also believed in secularism. Once, when Dr. Kalam was a student of class V, his teacher made him get up and sit apart from a Brahmin boy who was wearing the sacred thread. The boy and friend of Kalam Sri Ramanand Shastri, felt very sorry for this issue. When the father of Ramanand Shastri came to know about it, he called the teacher to his house and denounced this act and feelings of caste and creed and cautioned him not to repeat it in future. This left a strong influence on the subconscious mind of young Kalam and secularism established strong roots in his heart.

Dr. Kalam lived in a society of people from different castes. His science teacher Pandit Shiva Subramanian Iyer was a staunch orthodox Brahmin. He liked Abdul Kalam very much and used to tell him, "Kalam, I want to make you a man of dignity and fame both within and outside the country and that you should be recognized as a highly educated person in big cities." One day he invited Kalam to dine at his house. His wife was a very orthodox Brahmin lady who did not like to feed Kalam in her sacred place— kitchen. Panditjee served the meal to Kalam outside the kitchen and fed him with great love and affection and he also ate his meal in the same place. Panditjee did not take the matter seriously and made her understand that it takes time in changing the existing practices. After a week Kalam was again invited for dinner. When he went there, he found that the wife of his teacher was no more an orthodox lady, who herself took Kalam to the kitchen and served the meal with her own hands. On finding the change, Kalam developed more affection and respect for her.

Dr. Kalam adopted vegetarianism. He relished traditional Aiyyangar food like Vendhya Kozhambu and Puliyodare. But how did he embrace vegetarianism? Turns out that it was a well deciphered and practical choice. Turning into a vegetarian was one of many practical decisions he made in his life. The secret behind this conversion was opened by Dr. Kalam himself. During 1950's when he joined St. Joseph's College, Tiruchirappalli on a scholarship and within within students' budget, non-vegetarian meals was unaffordable. "Economy forced me to become a vegetarian, but I finally started liking it. Today I am 100 per cent vegetarian. Wherever I go, as long as I get a hot vegetable dish, I am okay. If I am in Gujarat, I have Gujarati food, if it's Shillong, it's North Eastern" Dr. Kalam quoted in one of his interviews to a daily.

Once Dr. Kalam's college friends and colleagues quoted a few interesting memories of old days with him. R. Aravamudan, former director, ISRO's Satellite Centre, Bangalore stated "We lived in Indira Bhavan Lodge in Thiruvananthapuram. People there called him Kalam Iyer because he moved around with Brahmins and had similar eating habits. The only non-vegetarian food he ate occasionally was egg masala along with Kerala parottas."

R Aravamudan first met A P J Abdul Kalam in 1963 at the National Aeronautics Space Agency, Wallops Island launching facility in Virginia, United States. There was a hostel attached to the station which had a self-service cafeteria. He said, "We lived mainly on mashed potatoes, boiled beans or peas, bread and lots of milk. Weekends were a whirl with supermarket shopping, visits to the cinema, and the occasional dinner at an Indian home."

Once they came back to India in 1964 and were stationed in Trivandrum for the setting up of the Thumba Rocket Station. Both Dr. Kalam and Aravamudan would take a ten minute walk daily to visit railway station in hope of getting some non-Keralite South Indian meal. Thumba station had no canteen of its own and the nearby areas had very limited eating options. So the two was mostly depended on the railway station for most of their meals.

If one really wants to know what this humble scientist liked, simply head to Annalakshmi Restaurant in Anna Salai, Chennai. He was a regular at this small eatery before he began his term as the 11th President of India. According to the management of this restaurant, his favourite dish here was Vatha Kuzhambu and Papad. Dr. Kalam also spent close to three decades of his life in Kerala's capital, Trivandrum. He graced the place with his presence between the 1960's and 80's. Here, one can visit the small, local, vegetarian restaurant named 'Guruvayoorappa' which has pictures of Dr. Kalam all over. The owner claims that he used to visit the restaurant almost every day back then.

When Kalam was a student at Madras Institute of Technology (MIT), he got an opportunity to structure a fighter plane used in war. His professor Srinivasan was not very happy with the pace of work. Kalam requested an extension of thirty days.

"Kalam, I have just three days to allot you. Make it or forget it," the professor warned.

Kalam forgot everything and devoted two days in preparing the drawings of the fighter plane. The professor was overwhelmed to see his student's dedication and embraced him tightly.

"I knew you would do it," the professor said.

Such was the commitment, dedication, and determination Kalam displayed for the projects he unndertook in his life.

After the Second World War when Kalam's father was sending him to the high school at Ramanathapuram, he was moved and he said to Kalam— "Abdul, since you are to progress in life so it is necessary to send you out. Our love will not confine you here." Seeing his mother's feeling, he encouraged her and said, "Your sons and daughters are not only yours but those of God. They have appeared in the world through you but they are actually sent by God." At the same time he said, "Abdul, if you are firm in your faith and devotion you will be able to change your fate." These thoughts of his father helped him to establish himself as a strong pillar.

During his childhood, the priest of lord Shiva's temple, Panchi

Shastri, used to say, "Kalam, always search for the truth because the truth only will help you to gather strength for your prosperity."

A teacher of Ramanathapuram Swartz High School always used to say, "An intelligent student can learn several times more than what a weak student can learn from a skilled teacher." Abdul Kalam liked this version very much. This is why he never harboured any weakness in his mind.

Strong will, faith and aspiration were embedded in the personality of Dr. Kalam. He knew that strong will is necessary for achievement. Dr. Kalam has mentioned in his autobiography—"During my childhood the flying birds in the sky attracted me to think about the mysteries of flight. I used to think as to how the birds can fly. Can I also fly? How will I feel if I could also fly?" And with this intense desire in his heart, Dr. Kalam was not only associated with the technicalities of flight but he also became a great inventor and a famous scientist.

Prof. Sarabhai believed that 'we not only learn from our mistakes but they offer us the chances for our betterment. New ideas are born in our mind.' At that time, a branch of Rocket Engineering and Laboratory was opened. Dr. Kalam used to remember the great personality—Prof. Sarabhai.

During his student days Dr. Kalam had strong desire to read the literature of Tolstoy, Tagore, Scott and Thomas Hardy. Though he was deeply interested in Physics, Philosophy was his second love, a subject which was always liked by him.

Dr. Kalam believed that 'an atom is movable and after sometime it is transformed. Science and God are not indifferent to each other but science is the inquisitiveness which comes out of heart which leads towards God.' Dr. Kalam tried to see science with the eye of spirituality.

Dr. Kalam often repeated the words of Pandit Nehru and Prof. Sarabhai and says that "If the people of India want to play an important role in the world, they must adopt a new technique to make progress."

Dr. Kalam has said in his autobiography: "The work done

without enthusiasm is like the food which can fill the belly but cannot give satisfaction. To the contrary, the meal prepared with affection gives full satisfaction. Like this, tenacity and enthusiasm are necessary to perform a great work, due to which a man achieves his objective easily."

Dr. Kalam still remember the sad demise of his brother- in-law and bosom friend and the agony he faced when he reached Rameshwaram. At that time his father encouraged him by saying—"Don't you see, how God spreads the darkness? But He has created sun also to show the path."

It has been said that the character of a man is not built by the association he keeps; rather it depends on how he can detach himself from a specific bad event or association. Dr. Kalam lived with the people who were senior to him in age. The association with the people having knowledge and culture had taught him during his youth that to lead a correct path the mind needs good thoughts. Knowledge has the capacity to make a man powerful if it is applied continuously in life.

Dr. Kalam had inherited refined culture which was a ladder of success. At the same time Dr. Kalam's life is the source of inspiration for the coming generations to show that a man does not become great by the chair he holds, but by his noble nature.

Glimpse of Hope in Despair

Dr. Kalam's life has experienced many ups and downs. His life was full of sorrows and difficulties as well as happiness. But he was never hesitant, he continued relentlessly on his way to progress. He worked hard for success. He took his failures to be ordained by God. He always remembered the version of his father—"God helps him who goes ahead with his work and duty and never misleads himself."

Dr. Kalam always remembered his ideology which helped him to reach the greatest peak of his progress. Dr. Kalam says, "I have learnt something or the other from my guardians, relatives, teachers, senior officers and colleagues."

Given below is a short introduction of his guardians, intimate friends and colleagues from whom he was inspired and became an eminent personality with the help of their support:

People in his life:

Abul Saheb

Abul Saheb was the great grandfather of Dr. Kalam. To pay him respect, Dr. Kalam has taken his first name 'Abul' -with his name.

Pakir Saheb

Pakir was grandfather of Dr. Kalam. This is also included in his name.

Jainulabaddin

Dr. Kalam's father was Jainulabaddin. His full name is Abul

Pakir Jainulabaddin Abdul Kalam. His father was a devout, benevolent and laborious person. These qualities were inherited by Dr. Kalam from his father.

Ashiyamma

Dr. Kalam had very close bonding with his mother Ashiyamma. He never forgot to mention eating rice and sambar with coconut chutney from his affectionate mother. He would say, "I often used to take food with my mother in the kitchen. She used to serve my favourite dish on banana leaf." She was not only an ideal life partner to his father but was also a brave lady. Dr. Kalam says about his parents' kindheartedness— "A person requires another man when he is in trouble that can help him to face the challenge. Whosoever comes to me during crisis, I always pray to god for them. My parents also had similar sentiments."

Ahmed Jalaluddin

Jalaluddin used to help Kalam's father in boat making work. Later he became his brother-in-law. While describing his brother-in law's kindness, he says—"He was not only a kind-hearted man but he had also profound belief in God. He always encouraged me to work for bright future." Jalaluddin was the foremost among his relatives who used to encourage Kalam to acquaint him about scholars, scientific discoveries and inventions, literature and other knowhow.

Johra

Johra was the elder sister of Dr. Kalam. He was very affectionate to his sister Johra. His beloved sister Johra had an ardent desire to see him a bloom into a renowned person. She arranged money for the admission fees and books after mortgaging her ornaments to get him admitted in M.I.T.

Dr. Kalam says that his family status was not rich enough to arrange immediate funds for getting admission in M.I.T. He needed one thousand rupees. Under such circumstances, his elder sister came to his rescue and she arranged for the money after mortgaging her ornaments including her chain and bangles. Dr. Kalam has not forgotten her sacrifice. As he says that he had taken the vow that he would repay that loan from the amount which he would get as his scholarship.

Shamsuddin

Shamsuddin was a cousin of Dr. Kalam. Shamsuddin made great contribution to Dr. Kalam's life. Dr. Kalam says that Shamsuddin was "my sympathizer, friend and brother during my childhood." Shamsuddin had a newspaper agency at Rameshwaram. Dr. Kalam used to get information regarding World War from the headlines of the newspapers. During IInd World War, in 1939, trains were not stopping at Rameshwaram station. Bundles of newspapers used to be dropped at Rameshwaram Road Station. Shamsuddin required an assistant to help him in the business. Kalam used to assist him.

Mustafa Kalam

Elder brother of Dr. Kalam, Mustafa was busy taking care of the family. There was a grocery store for family expenses. Kalam used to help him there. Demand of tamarind seeds increased during 2nd World War all of a sudden. He used to gather tamarind seeds from road side trees and used to sell those seeds in the shop which were situated in the Mosque's lane. There he used to earn one anna. This way he used to contribute financially at home.

Kasim Mohammad

Kalam was fond of multicolored artistic creations of the sea shell, conch shell and other items for decoration purpose which were available in a shop owned by his younger brother Kasim Mohammad. Many a time he used to pass time at that shop.

Pt. Laxman Shastri

Dr. Kalam had great respect for Pandit Laxman Shastri, the head priest of a Shiva temple of Rameshwaram. Dr. Kalam used to discuss spiritualism with him. Pandit Laxman Shastri used to preach him from the portion of 'Shrimad Bhagwat Geeta' about actions of human beings. He always preached Kalam that those who wanted truth had to search for it.

Shiv Subramanyam Iyer

The Science teacher of Kalam, Shiv Subramanian Iyer, was a true orthodox Brahmin but he loved him very much and used to call him at home for meal. Though his wife used to oppose it, he offered him meal with a lot of affection. He always told him— "Kalam, I want to see you as a great personality." No doubt, he reached a great height with the blessing of his teacher.

Annadorai Solomon

He was a respected teacher. He was very affectionate, open-minded and learned teacher. Apart from that he was an ideal guide for curious students. He always said, "A weak student can learn from a skilled teacher, an intelligent student can learn still better."

There are three strengths to get success and to have better result in life. These strengths are—will, faith and aspirations. According to his thoughts, Dr. Kalam says, "I wanted to know the secret of flying birds in the sky which inspired me to understand high flight."

Ramakrishna Iyer

He was a very disciplined and strict teacher. Once, Abdul Kalam was beaten by him due to some reason. When Kalam stood first, he told students, "See, when I beat someone, he gets good marks and becomes a great personality in future."

Dr. Kurt and Prof. Spender

While studying at M.I.T. these teachers were source of inspiration for Dr. Kalam. With their joint efforts Dr. Kalam became the best engineer. Prof. Spender taught him about aerodynamics and Dr. Kurt taught mechanical knowhow of aeronautics.

K.A.V. Pan Dalai

Dr. Kalam said Prof. K.A.V. Pan Dalai was a teacher as well as a friend of him. Every time he found something new in his teaching.

Kalam had been taught by him the subject of Aero structure design and analysis. He gave chance to every student to let him speak and he listened to them very carefully.

Prof. Narasimha Rao

Dr. Kalam always remembered Prof. Rao enthusiastically while mentioning Aerodynamics.

Prof. Rao was a Mathematics teacher in M.I.T. He used to go into minute details of Theoretical Aerodynamics to explain elaborately. Dr. Kalam accepted the fact that had Prof. Rao not been there it would not have been possible for him to understand the equation of Aerodynamics. His way of teaching was so simple that Dr. Kalam could choose Physics as main subject. In this way Dr. Kalam acquired knowledge of aerodynamics. He designed many new models of aeroplanes which included Bi-plane, Monoplane, Tail less plane and Delta wing aeroplanes were amongst them.

Prof. Srinivasan

A critical moment in Dr. Kalam's life came when he entered into 3rd and final year of M.I.T. and faced Prof. Srinivasan who was a Professor in Design. He was also the Director of M.I.T. He appointed Kalam and other classmates in design making project of fighter planes. Dr. Kalam was given the responsibility of Aerodynamics design and other four classmates were given topics like transmission, formation, control and equipments. After some time when Prof. Srinivasan came for inspection he was upset to see the progress of the project. Since it delayed, Kalam apologized and asked for one month time to finish that project in a systematic manner. After receiving his apology, Prof. Srinivasan warned him and said if he could not complete that job within three days then his scholarship would be stopped. This warning came as a great shock to him because the scholarship meant everything to him. His future was dependent on it. So applied himself with resolve to complete that project. Ultimately his hard labour bore fruit and he completed the project within three days. Prof. Srinivasan praised him after seeing his work.

V.K. Krishna Menon

Dr. Kalam produced wingless, light, supersonic Hovercraft and named it "Nandi". Defence Minister of that time Sri V.K. Krishna Menon was impressed. He took a ride of the Hovercraft and told Kalam in praise that he should create more powerful planes and call him for the next ride.

Prof. M.G.K. Menon

Prof Menon, the Director of Tata Institute of Fundamental Research, Mumbai wanted to take a ride when he heard about the Hovercraft. He reached Bangalore and took a ride. After flying he asked a few questions and returned back to Mumbai. After a week Dr. Kalam received a letter in which he was being called for an interview for the post of Rocket Engineer in Indian Space Research Organisation.

Prof. Oda

Every individual has some ups and downs in his life which he remembers throughout. Dr. Kalam's life is no exception. His past moments help us to understand him not only as a President but also to know the scientist: Dr. Kalam acknowledges that it is very natural for a man to get disappointment despite putting hard efforts.

Prof. Oda was a scientist in the Institute of Space and Aeronautical Sciences in Japan. Dr. Kalam remembered him as a great soul who was dedicated to his work. Once, Dr. Kalam was using his Timer Device along with Payload of Prof. Oda. At that time Prof Oda instructed him to attach Japanese make Timer Device though Japan-made Timer Device was inferior one in his view. Prof. Oda took for granted that Japan-made Timers were much better than Indian Timers. He accepted the suggestion and used Japan-made timers. Mission was not successful due to some glitches which cropped up in the Timers. Dr. Oda was very disturbed and shattered. Dr. Kalam could never forget such an emotional and industrious personality.

Prof. Sudhakar

Prof. Sudhakar was a colleague of Dr. Kalam in Payload project. Once Dr. Kalam and Prof. Sudhakar were studying the chemicals in Payload room. It was a humid and hot day at Thumba. Prof. Sudhakar was working with sodium and one drop of sweat fell into that chemical. There was a huge blast and fire broke out in the room. The fire of sodium can not be put with water. Prof. Sudhakar did not lose presence of mind in this critical situation. He broke window glasses and took out Dr. Kalam first and then he jumped out. His hand was badly injured but he faced it with smile.

Indira Gandhi at Thumba

To dedicate Thumba Equatorial Rocket Launching Station (T.E.R.L.S.) to U.N.O. Prime Minister Indira Gandhi visited Thumba in February 1969. She inaugurated the first-of- its-kind Filament Winding Machine of our country which was made in Dr. Kalam's laboratory. In the presence of Smt. Indira Gandhi, Dr. Kalam and his team members got congratulations and were cheered.

Jai Chandra Babu

RATO project work was going on in war footing. It had become normal practice to work till late hours at the office of Dr. Kalam. One official, Mr. Jai Chandra Babu, was working, in his office. Once Dr. Kalam asked him—"Could you make some suggestions on this project?" He explained two major hurdles of that project. He raised some points related to administration. Jai Chandra Babu discussed the issues pertaining to management and contractorship without any hesitation. At the same time he suggested Dr. Kalam to hand over the job of financial approvals to one person. The persons engaged in project-related work should get facility of air travel. One particular person should be answerable for job specification. Instruments and other parts should be brought in aeroplane. To bring the transparency in accounts of the organisation, private sector should be invited.

Dr. Kalam never heard such demands in the government departments. He took those suggestions seriously and put them in action.

Prof. Kurien

The development work of every single small phase was under observation in the team of Dr. Kalam. Though he was working collectively with his colleagues there was every possibility to commit some mistakes. Prof. Sarabhai decided to bring him in contact with Prof. Kurien. Dr. Prof. Kurien was chairman of Centre National Etudas Spatiales (C.N.E.S.) of Japan. After realizing the heavy work load of Dr. Kalam, Prof. Kurien advised Prof. Sarabhai to relieve Dr. Kalam from small and light projects and to hand over more important projects to him. Kalam was relieved from small and less important projects and engaged in 4th phase of Diamont Airframe work. Though Diamont Airframe and S.L.V. were different, this was a new type of project. His colleagues had cautioned him before accepting that responsibility.He completed the job.

It took one year to complete Diamant Airframe programme after doing research work on personal advice, design and the construction for some time.

Dr. Werner Van Braun

Dr. Kalam got an opportunity to meet not only a renowned and great scientist in Rocket science but also a legend in the history of Missile technology and no one was above him in that field. He was none other than Dr. Werner Van Braun, who had made V-2 Missile during 2nd World War and devastating attack was made through these missiles on London. Later he was called by NASA. He made Jupiter missiles for America. He was appointed as director in German Missiles Programme. Dr. Kalam says about him, "I could not imagine that he would be so polite and inspiring." Dr. Werner Van Braun said to Dr. Kalam, "You should remember that we not only come up with our success but failures also bring development.

It is not enough to do hard labour in Rocket Technology but to determine to reach target is also necessary and this determination comes only when we take this science as religion, not profession." This thought of Dr. Braun influenced Dr. Kalam and he started to take it as spiritual matter.

Journey As A Scientist

Abdul Kalam had always aspired to become a fighter pilot. It was one of his most cherished dreams. After specialising in aeronautical engineering from Madras Institute of Technology, Kalam was excited to pursue a career in flying. Over the years he had nurtured the hope to be able to fly to handle a machine that rose higher in the sky. One of the interview calls Mr. Kalam got was from the Indian Air Force in Dehradun. The other was from the Directorate of Technical Development and Production (DTDP) at the Ministry of Defence in New Delhi. Although the interview at DTDP was quite easy, the authorities were looking for certain level of smartness in their candidate. It was considered along with the qualifications and engineering knowledge he possessed. So Mr. Kalam bagged the ninth position out of 25 candidates and could not get recruited owing to availability of just 8 slots.

"I had failed to realise my dream of becoming an air force pilot," Abdul Kalam wrote in one of his books.

While moving to Dehradun, he was walking around with his parents' hopes and aspirations loaded in the baggage. The fate had something else in store. Kalam travelled his way to Rishikesh and aimed towards starting a new life. The abode of holy Ganges welcomed him with open arms. After taking up the job as the senior scientific assistant at DTDP half-heartedly, little did he know the bigger things fate was ready to award him with. After graduation, he joined India's Defence Research and Development Organization (DRDO) to work on a hovercraft project. His dedication and commitment to work was highly appreciated by his seniors. Kalam then joined Indian Space Research Organisation (ISRO) in 1963. At ISRO, he initiated fibre reinforced plastics activities. He later joined the Satellite Launch Vehicle team at Thumba and became the Project Director for SLV-3. He has made significant contributions to the Indian Satellite Launch Vehicle.

Once during his childhood, Kalam visited a temple with his friend to watch Ramlila. There, he got impressed by one of the rockets. As time passed though, rockets were turned into a deep passion for Kalam. He started making new rockets and flying them whenever there was spare time in hand. While going through some of the literary works dedicated to rockets and other artillery collection used across the world, Kalam came across a book on Tipu Sultan. It said that the emperor from Mysore created the first rocket. This impressed Kalam and he started exploring more on this subject. The scientist also scrolled through a lot of epics, holy books, and granthas to pacify his inquisitiveness. His dream turned true when he got an opportunity to work with Dr. Vikram Sarabhai, the Father of the Indian space program and founder of ISRO (Indian Space Research Organization). In the year 1962, Kalam joined ISRO. This initiated a never ending saga of success. The scientist learnt a lot from this association. Kalam was a project director of the Rohini satellite program under the guidance of Sarabhai. While putting his engineering expertise to brilliant use, he learnt crucial aspects of leadership from some of the best leaders across the globe including Dr. Vikram Sarabhai, Prof. Satish Dhawan, and Dr Brahm Prakash.

Dr. Vikram Sarabhai was impressed by Kalam's spirit and enthusiasm towards work. He did his best to promote Kalam. Aeronautical Development Establishment (ADE) was established in January 1959 at High Grounds, Bangalore. Sarabhai appointed Kalam in this branch. He kept polishing his skills by introducing new struggles. Once Sarabhai had given him a challenging task of creating a device 'RATO' in just 18 months. This device was supposed to carry load and help fighter planes stay operational under adverse situations during war. When Sarabhai decided to create devices with advanced projection and launching techniques, Dr. Kalam offered to lead the project under his expert guidance. Kalam's mentor and friend Dr. Vikram Sarabhai, the Father of

Indian Space Science played a significant role in shaping his career and making him the 'Missile Man' of India.

Kalam's friends have always stood by his side. When the ministry of Defence constituted a missile panel, Kalam was appointed as the project leader. The panel also had V.S. Narayanan as Group Captain, Dr. V.R. Gowarikar, M.R. Kurup and A.E. Muthunayagam as members. The Indian Space Research Organisation (ISRO) was created and Kalam was handpicked by Vikram Sarabhai, India's space pioneer, as the project manager of a team that would build India's first satellite launch vehicle (SLV). In 1969 Kalam enjoyed his first stint with aerospace engineering. He assumed the position of Project director of India's first Satellite Launch Vehicle (SLV-III) at Indian Space Research Organisation (ISRO). This vehicle launched the Rohini satellite in 1980. SLV was intended to reach a height of 400 km and carry a payload of 40 kg. The first experimental flight of SLV-3 conducted in August 1979, was only partially successful. This was precisely a four-stage rocket with all solid-propellant motors.

In the year 1979, SLV was first launched. The fourth and final launch of the SLV took place on 17th April 1983. Kalam led Integrated Guided Missile Development Programme of India. It was under his expert supervision that the short and medium-range ballistic missile projects named Prithvi and Agni were successfully completed.

Kalam along with DRDO chief V S Arunachalam presented their plan to to defence minister R Venkataraman with an aim to make India self-sufficient in missile systems. Their proposal was to successively develop five enormous missile systems from scratch : the anti-tank guided missile Nag, a surface-to-surface missile of 150 km range later named Prithvi, surface-to air missiles the tactical Trishul and Akash, and Kalam's pet project Agni. The overall concept of Agn was drawn from his favourite re-entry experiment (REX) project at ISRO. The development of these missiles helped India emerge as one among developed nations across the globe armed with technologically advanced nuclear weapons and tools. As the Scientific advisor to the Ministry of Defence and the Secretary to the Department of Defence Research and Development, he designed the concept of joint partnership which led to the formation of BrahMos Aerospace between Russia and India.

The massive 2100 acre land of DRDO was allotted for the establishment of RCI in 1970's for the purpose of Anti Tank Missile Testing. Dr A.P.J. Abdul Kalam the then Director of DRDL persuaded Govt of Andhra Pradesh to do so. RCI is 'Avionics Hub' of DRDO. It also serves as one of the three DRDO Labs of 'Missile Complex'. It is home to varied operation centers, integration and testing facilities. RCI serves as the leading lab for Defence Research Development Organization (DRDO) and responsible for development of missile system. It is also used for design, development and participation in production of missile avionics.

Kalam served as the Chief Scientific Adviser to the Prime Minister and the Secretary of the Defence Research and Development Organisation from July 1992 to December 1999. The Pokhran-II nuclear tests were conducted during this period in which he played an intensive political and technological role under Atal Bihari Vajpayee Government. Dr. Kalam had said while delivering the 7th RN KAO Memorial Lecture organized by the Research and Analysis Wing (RAW) that India launched a series of missiles, rockets and dropped experimental bombs to divert attention of 'snoopers' prior to conducting the 1998 nuclear tests. The great scientist admitted that these well-planned measures were taken with an aim to 'divert the attention of snoopers' two days before the nuclear tests in Pokhran during the summer of 1998. He also mentioned about the anxious days prior to the nuclear tests during which the DRDO and his team worked over-time so as to make the tests successful in utter secrecy.

APJ Abdul Kalam also admitted that PV Narasimha Rao had asked him to make preparations for nuclear tests. For a crucial event that was to take place the following day, multiple agencies were in action. The next two nights were dark nights with no moon light. The other side, the world was sleeping. At the Chandipur flight test range, a series of 12 Trishuls were launched. It was calculated as one launch in every two hours. At the Island range at stealth launch pad, a simulated Agni launch preparations went on in high intensity. Several rockets of PINAKA type were put into action in Pokharan ranges. Thereafter, at mid-day and evening, Air Force aircraft started bombarding with runway destruction bombs on experimental runways. The following day, India woke up to the news that three nuclear tests had been conducted on the same day and another two the next day.

In his speech, Kalam had said, "No one knew about it except three souls and their classified team...the whole event I described can be classified as more than a Black Swan."

On 11th May 1998 and 13th May 1998, Operation Shakti (Pokhran-II) was initiated with the detonation of one fusion and two fission bombs. This helped the Indian government led by Prime Minister Atal Bihari Vajpayee declare India a full-fledged nuclear state officially.

Dr. Kalam took up academic pursuit as Professor, Technology & Societal Transformation at Anna University, Chennai from November 2001 and was involved in teaching and research tasks. Above all he took up a mission to ignite the young minds for national development by meeting over 1 lakh high school students across the country.

Dr. Kalam had a mission behind every step he took in life. All of his plans would revolve around these missions. In one of his excellent literary works India '2020', Kalam had mentioned, "India is a knowledge superpower and developed nation." Dr. Kalam has also given a brief about different ways to develop India by 2020. He has set up an intelligent target for all the youth in India on making India developed by the year 2020. Kalam has also said that it should be the dream of all citizens to see India a developed country, only then the dream would come true.

As a workaholic, Kalam used to work for 18 hours a day.

Learning new things and spreading knowledge was among one of his passions. According to Professor M.G.K. Menon, Dr. Kalam was a man of rare intelligence with a passion to learn and discover deep secrets of science. This great scientist was always a learner, and excited and willing to learn new things.

Promise of Devotion

Dr. Abdul Kalam once again reaffirmed before the world that hard work with patience and quiet resolve make a man successful. Tenacity and firm determination are also required for completion of mission. Dr. Kalam says in his autobiography, "I started accepting the matters and events the way they came in my life. Neither M.G.K. Menon would have come to Bangalore on tour nor I could have gone to Mumbai for the post of Rocket Engineer on behalf of Indian Committee for Space Research!" It was a new beginning in the life of Dr. Kalam to do work in Space Research Committee in Mumbai.

In the mid 1962, it was decided to establish a Rocket Launching Centre by Indian Space Research Organization at Thumba village of Tiruvanthapuram in Kerala. Because Thumba village lies close to the magnetic axis of the earth it was chosen for rocket launching. A big church is situated in that area. Dr. Kalam admits that he got a lot of cooperation from the Bishop of that Church, Father Dr. Derira, for establishment of the rocket launching centre. With his help, it was possible to open an office of Thumba space centre at the church premises. Dr. Kalam experienced the inner eternal strength while working there.

For the first time Dr. Kalam could get technical know- how of computer through computer training at that temporary space centre. After that he was sent to the topmost space research institute "National Aeronautics and Space Administration" i.e. NASA in U.S.A. for training to get acquainted with the latest technology of rocket launching.

'NASA' is the biggest Institute in the world in space research.

Dr. Kalam could gain some experience after putting 6 months over there. His training started from Langlay Research Centre which was near Hampton city of Virginia state. After completion of his work he was sent to Guide Space Flight Centre at Greenbelt of Maryland state. The development and construction of satellites are done there. Dr. Kalam reached his destination where the main base of American Rocket programme was situated where he gathered all the knowledge, technical knowhow. The place was on the Eastern Coast of Zirnia called "Valep Flight Facility".

Dr. Kalam was attracted by seeing a painting of soldiers of Tipu Sultan at the reception room of that centre. It was the painting of a war scene in which some rockets were flying. When Dr. Kalam asked about that painting, he was told by the officers of the institute that the soldiers of Tipu Sultan attacked the British soldiers with rockets. Immediately Dr. Kalam could understand that Tipu Sultan already had discovered rockets in his time which was useful for face to face fighting. Dr. Kalam was so happy to see the past glory of our country in a foreign land and after watching the ancient rockets he started imagining modern rockets.

Dr. Kalam returned to India after completing his training. The first rocket "Nike Apache" was launched on 21st November 1963 from Thumba. This is the place where Dr. Kalam performed an important role to give final shape of this programme. Now, this place is converted into Indian Space Museum.

Prior to the first rocket launching, there was an interesting incident. The rocket was placed in the church building, which has been mentioned earlier. This rocket was loaded on the truck and taken to the launching site. It had to be erected on launcher after lifting it with the help of a crane. But since the crane had broken down, the rocket was coming down instead of going upward. Dr. Kalam had taken responsibility to launch it in given time. It was not possible either to repair that crane or to search for an alternative. Dr. Kalam faced that critical situation with patience and lifted the rocket on shoulder with the help of colleagues and located it on the launcher. Rocket was launched successfully on time. The moment the rocket touched the height of the sky Dr. Kalam and his team members were very cheerful.

Next day Dr. Vikram Sarabhai called him for discussion for further programme. Dr. Kalam has mentioned about Prof. Sarabhai that he was not only a man of supernatural strength but also he used to deliver new methods of working to the young engineers and scientists. He encouraged them. Prof. Sarabhai used to believe in competency rather than the educational qualifications of engineers and scientists.

Prof. Sarabhai was very enthusiastic after the successful launching of "Nike Apache" and decided to make his next successful satellite for the country. He explained the project to Dr. Kalam and his team members enthused them. Prof. Sarabhai got himself busy with other programmes for development of the rocket. Physical Research Laboratory was immediately set up at Ahmedabad and the programmes for development of scientific instruments were started on war footing.

To start with, one sounding rocket was manufactured in India. This rocket 'Rohini', while going around the earth in the atmosphere, was planned to inform about weather. This way of manufacturing rocket started in India. After Rohini, 'Menaka' was manufactured. The credit of the achievement also goes to Dr. Kalam and his team members for their hard work. It is clear that these challenges and responsibility strengthened till then Indian pay-load was launched through French rockets, now Indian rockets are used for launching.

His marvellous achievements earned Dr. Kalam the reputation of being the 2nd seniormost scientist after Prof. Sarabhai.

Creation of National Rocket

'Rohini' rocket was launched on 20th November 1967. A solid motor, weighing 32 kg, was fitted and to establish it at 10 kilometre height a 7 kilogram pay-load was attached with it. After some time one more rocket was launched in which two solid motors and 100 kilogram pay-load was given for 350 kilometre height and launched. Continuous development of these rockets put Indian scientists on a path of progress and at the same time they moved from strength to strength in their expertise in the field of missiles.

After this success, time was ripe to build RATO (Rocket Assisted Take off System) motor for manufacturing of rocket in India. Since this job had to be completed under the patronage of Prof. Sarabhai, he wanted to hand over this responsibility to Dr. Kalam. Prof Sarabhai called Dr. Kalam and Group Captain V.S. Narayan of Air Force to Delhi in this context. Dr. Abdul Kalam and V.S. Narayan met him at Delhi as scheduled.

Prof Sarabhai put the proposal of the forthcoming project of RATO motors before them and took them to show the RATO motor which was brought from Russia.

"If I order for such motors from Russia, can you make same motors here?" Dr. Kalam and V.S. Narayan did not have any doubts on the proposal of Dr. Sarabhai. They gave positive answer to him and they busied themselves in making the motor as per programme along with other team members. Only 1 1/2 years were allotted for the completion of the task. Prof Sarabhai informed Prime Minister Indira Gandhi about the new project and the manufacturing of the indigenous RATO motors were announced.

Potentiality of RATO

RATO motor is a special type of motor which is not only powerful but can also make flight in critical condition. These motors are being used in Air Force planes. RATO motors are proved to be conducive for producing more energy and they can move higher. RATO is capable of facing any situation since the fighter planes of the Air Force are meant for bombarding. As they were likely to break down very quickly and had to take off and take across planes on unsuitable runway during critical condition, RATO can surmount all these eventualities. RATO motor can lift maximum weight and can perform better in higher temperature.

It was necessary to have more RATO motors for S-22 and HF-24 planes of Indian Air Force. Russian made motor was a heavy weight of 225 kilograms and was capable to take 3000 kilogram load with speed and could go upwards successfully in which dual transmissions were attached.

Now it was time for country-made RATO motor development after studying the Russian made RATO motor. It was planned to hand over the development and manufacturing of that motor to Space Science and Technology Centre with the assistance of Indian Air Force headquarters. The alloy that was to be used in instrumentation was yet to be finalized. It was essential to develop powerful fuel usage and also complete other related work. After thorough research and study Dr. Kalam came to the conclusion that fibre glass and composing propellent could be used in place of metal and fuel respectively to get successful results.

Work was started after making a blue print for the project. In the meantime,two other projects also commenced. The first one was related to modus operandi of Space Research and the second one was for launching of satellite in the orbit of earth i.e. making the Satellite Launching Vehicle (SLV). It was a great dream for a sagacious scientist like Prof. Sarabhai. A team under Dr. Kalam was engaged to give a well defined shape to the work. One panel was set up for the development work of different types of missiles in which Dr. Kalam and Group Captain V.S. Narayan were included. To manufacture missile in India was a great breakthrough and also a big challenge before Indian scientists. Continuous efforts in research work yielded some fruits and Dr. Kalam came into limelight as the "Missile Man" on world map. Instruments for missiles used to be imported. Now they were manufactured in India itself.

The development work of RATO progressed so fast that it finished before time i.e. within one year. Indian-made RATO cost only Rs 17,000 whereas foreign made motor was cost Rs 330,000 rupees. Now Dr. Kalam was on the headline of newspapers for his achievements. He proved the proverb that winners always do differently. This different way becomes essence of success.

New Trails in the Horizon

Prof. Vikram Sarabhai put continuous efforts for the development of SLV (Space Launching Vehicle) till he reaped the benefits of space technology in 1969. For that purpose he made survey and started visiting many places where it can be launched. Prof Sarabhai paid more attention in the coastal region of east because launching vehicle could get maximum support to rotate from west to east around the earth. To give final shape of the purpose, 'Indian Rocket Society' was reorganized to bring together personalities engaged in this field.

Immediately, one advisory committee was formed under Defence Ministry. Indian Space Research Organisation was established to work under the supervision of Atomic Energy Commission. Responsibility was given to ISRO for research work on the space science. Entire project was divided into four stages and for each stage one scientist was appointed. Dr. Kalam was responsible for making designs which was in fourth stage. It is necessary to mention that Dr. Kalam had to prepare a composite structure. Though Dr. Kalam had full cooperation of Prof Sarabhai, this was his acid test.

Dr. Kalam utilized his knowledge and experience in this job and thus, the structure was ready before time, whereas other three stages took 5 years to complete. Dr. Kalam proved that hard work and discipline not only bring perfection in timeliness but the results are also of a very high quality.

By 1968, Thumba had developed the capacity of manufacturing all the parts of the aircraft indigenously. Meanwhile Prof. Sarabhai reached Thumba where he had to demonstrate the system of separating the front part of the rocket from the rest of the structure by explosion. Dr. Kalam requested him to push the switch to inaugurate the thermal system.

Prof. Sarabhai pushed the switch, but the system did not work. All the scientists present were taken aback for a while. Dr. Kalam thought of activating the system straightway to the circuit by removing the timer. As soon as he did so, the system got started. Prof. Sarabhai was happy to see the success of Dr. Kalam and his associates but this incidence also provoked him to set up the 'Rocket Engineering Department' which could solve such sudden and unexpected problems.

Prof. Sarabhai believed that our mistakes teach us to correct ourselves and if the mistakes are not rectified immediately, we can fall down to abysmal depths. In fact this mistake would not have happened if the wrong connection had been detected earlier.

Regular meetings of the Missile Panel started taking place to avoid any such mishaps in future. Dr. Kalam used to convey the details of all the meetings to Prof. Sarabhai. On 30th of December 1971 he gave all the detailed information to Prof. Sarabhai after which he was directed to see Prof. Sarabhai at the Trivandrum airport. But destiny willed otherwise. Prof. Sarabhai suffered a heart-attack hours after he had a talk with Dr. Kalam and passed away. This unexpected incidence shocked Dr. Kalam . He had lost his revered Guru, guide and mantor. The nation had lost the father of the Indian Space Science. Dr. Kalam compared him with the father of the nation.

Prof. Vikram Sarabhai and
Dr. Kalam

Prof. Vikram Sarabhai, who had dreamt to conquer the space is no more but to realise his dreams continues to be a matter of serious pursuit in ISRO even today. Dr. Kalam took him as his guide. When he was alive, he dedicated all his success and the heights he achieved to Prof. Sarabhai who was a brilliant. Dr Kalam remembered him very fondly.

Prof Sarabhai had proposed Dr. Kalam's name as the trainee candidate to NASA for the modern technical training of Rocket Launching. Prof. Sarabhai assessed the capability of an engineer or a scientist not by his degree or by his training but by his self-confidence.

Prof. Sarabhai had the keen desire that India must be independent in rocket manufacturing and hence he was always full of zeal to launch new initiatives.

He always gave new technical knowledge to the engineers and when it reflected in their work his face was lit with joy.

He was never shaken even in adverse situations, instead he accepted that to err or to forget something in order to learn something is natural and not an offence.

He said that if we want to establish ourselves in the world, we have to be self-sufficient and search for new ideas and techniques.

He communicated about the entire new project to him and started working on it only after having discussed it with everyone.

He said that the performers must have physical as well as

emotional attachment with the project otherwise he cannot devote himself to it.

If he was not satisfied with the work of any engineer or any scientist, he immediately told him about his fault in a very clear way and at the same time he was very positive at such moments.

He said that failures make us more steadfast and composed as compared to successes.

Professor Dr. Vikram Sarabhai died of a heart attack on 30th of December, 1971. The sudden death of this great scientist at the early age of 52 years was a big setback to the Indian science fraternity. A meeting between him and Dr. Kalam was fixed for the same date but unfortunately it could not take place.

Dr. Kalam has stated that he was influenced the most by Prof. Sarabhai during his tenure.

When he talked of the interview for the post of rocket engineer in the Space Research Centre he said that the greatness of Prof. Sarabhai was perceptible from his politeness. Neither he was influenced by bureaucracy nor did he have any pride of his greatness. He always looked like a simple man. Prof. Sarabhai was not only an idol but also a guide for him. The credit for sending him for training of rocket launching in the National Aeronautics and Space Administration (NASA) in America goes to Prof. Sarabhai as Dr. Kalam was sent to NASA on his recommendation.

Dr. Kalam says that Prof. Sarabhai was such a genius that he could very quickly solve any problem. He was in the habit of giving new tips to young engineers. To keep normal even in adverse situation was his nature. His inclination to do something new every time had made him popular among others. This is why Dr. Kalam and his associates became very happy whenever they got the information of Prof. Sarabhai's visit to Thumba. He lent an expert hand in solving the problems experienced by Dr. Kalam during space research. This resulted in good co-operation from talented scientists of the institute. The launch of satellite SLV was possible in India and the inspiration from Prof. Vikram Sarabhai was largely responsible for this feat. It will not be an exaggeration to say that Prof. Sarabhai is like a Sun shining over the horizon of Indian Science which would keep showing light to the future generations of scientists.

Dr. Kalam talked of a very particular quality of Prof. Sarabhai and said that he explained all his decisions and future programmes to his colleagues. He did not like to keep secrets. He also firmly believed that failures show us the way to success. Dr. Kalam followed his footsteps throughout his life

SLV-III Project

Prof. Satish Dhawan was made the president of ISRO after the death of Prof. Sarabhai. All the organizations in Thumba such as space Science and Technology Centre, Rocket Propellant Plant, Rocket Fabrication Facility and the Propellant Fuel Complex were merged to form a complete space centre which was named 'Vikram Sarabhai Space Centre'. Famous metallurgist, Dr. Brahmaprakash, was appointed as the Director of the Centre.

The SLV project was in full bloom in Vikram Sarabhai Space Centre. All the sub-channels had been developed. Now only internal co-ordination was required. Prof. Dhawan had selected Dr. Kalam for successful functioning of the project. Dr. Kalam was in high spirits but at the same time he was a little worried with the thought of how he would be able to perform his duty among so many senior scientists who were working with him.

Dr. Kalam never took credit for any of his successes but credited of all the senior and dutiful colleagues with it. A great believer in 'Work is worship', he liked to concentrate on work. With his humble nature ,he had become a favourite of his co-workers.

His biography reveals his dedication to work. He says, "I went into the laboratory forgetting all the difficulties and criticisms in the same way as my father went into the mosque taking off the shoes."

The whole SLV project was to be completed within five and a half years. Dr. Kalam divided the whole project into three phases. Although he had to face many difficulties during this period, he paid no heed and continued his job with patience which he had learnt from his father. He used to say, "The destiny tests a man in many ways. In such situations patience is the first step to success."

One of the three phases divided by Dr. Kalam was management, upkeep and supervision; the second was related to the technical minutes of the project and the third, the most important, was to develop sub-channels. Engineers namely Madhavan Nayar, Ved Prakash Sandlas, S. Srinivasan, M.S.R Deo, Sunderrajan, U.S. Singh, Abdul Majeed, Shashi Kumar and Nambudiri extended their full co-operation to Dr. Kalam. Cheerful atmosphere and tendency to praise each other had brought all the engineers very close to each other to face the challenge of the project.

Dr. Kalam got up very early in the morning. It had become his routine to chalk out the day's programme after taking the morning walk. He always tried to finish at least two or three assignments in a day. He opted for the works which could be finished in less time and then he looked into the unfinished and pending work. In the end he took up the charge of important tasks.

During the period of designing of SLV-3, about 250 subparts and 40 sub-systems were prepared. There were almost 1 million parts , each different than other, required for the project. Importance was given to the products made by private manufacturers. Private vendors were asked to manufacture parts so that their technical skill could be developed and also they, the Indian industrialists would start developing interest in Indian Space Mission's component requirements.

Designing of SLV-3 and manufacturing of ground-to-air missile in DRDO were still in process when suddenly the project of RATO Motor manufacturing was stopped. This was so because the planes that were imported did not require RATO motor. This project was replaced by another project named Devil, under which the indigenous motor was to be developed to produce ground-to-air missiles. Dr. Kalam was made rocket scientist of this project.

SLV-3: A Knowhow

The composition of the front part of the SLV which has the

Pride of the Nation: Dr. A.P.J. Abdul Kalam

control system and the pilotage system is as complex as the human brain. This brain of the plane is fitted with electronic systems. It has arms of the size of human being   in the form of induction which is made up of metals or non-metals like stainless steel, aluminum, magnesium, titanium, beryllium, tungsten etc. Apart from this there are some unified mixtures which are not soluble being different from each other.

Some may be carbonic, some non-carbonic whereas some matters are of unlimited structure. Dr. Kalam used variety of glass pieces to strengthen plastic. A complex current is set up in the SLV which provides energy to its mechanical structure. This energy increases the speed of the plane. Aeronautic systems like digital electronics, microwave radar and transponder were being worked on from earlier. Meanwhile physical conditions in the SLA like pressure, vibration, conduction etc. started being measured.

Physical dimensions of the plane are converted into electronic symbols. Then the remote measurement system sends them to the earth in the form of radio waves. If there is any fault in these systems, the plane is immediately destroyed. Therefore to ensure maximum security a remote control system was developed so that in any such calamity the plane could easily be destroyed. This system was named 'interferometer.' In this way Dr. Kalam proved Earl Nightingale's words : 'Success is to attain the valuable goals. Success is only a journey, not a destination. After attaining one goal we have the second, the third, and the fourth and so on to achieve.'

The First Step of Success

The last step of the SLV project was almost completed. Dr. Kalam was determined to complete this project at the earliest. The modus operandi was divided into three categories. Till 1975 all the sub-systems were being developed by sounding rockets and were being made fit for the flight. In 1976 the sub-orbital flight and by 1978 the final take off of SLV was to take place.

The work related to the first step was in progress. Suddenly Dr. Kalam was informed that his guide, friend and brother-in-law, Jalaluddin had died in Rameshwaram. His cousin, Ahmed Jalaluddin was his first mentor who had lot of trust and faith in APJ and always motivated him to pursue good education.

Barely had he recovered from this shock , he got another jolt . His father had passed away at the age of 102. He had immense love and respect for his Father who was a simple man. He always said

'Whenever human beings find themselves alone, as a natural reaction, they start looking for company. Whenever they are in trouble, they look for someone to help them...Every recurrent anguish, longing and desire finds it own special helper. For the people who come to me in distress, I am but a go-between in their effort to ward off demonic forces with prayers and offerings....One must understand the difference between a fear-ridden vision of destiny and the vision that enables us to seek the enemy of fulfillment within ourselves...When troubles come, try to understand the relevance of your sufferings. Adversity always presents opportunities for introspection.'

These two misfortunes one after the other had shaken him very deeply. Those days he had to go to France where an Indian rocket, developed in France, was to be tested. The news of the sudden death of his mother plunged him in sorrow.

He was alone in the whole world. When he went to the funeral ceremony he could hear his father was telling him,

"Your mother has very honestly carried out all the responsibilities I had assigned to her. Don't mourn her death, concentrate on your work." This silent advice helped him to stand up again. Now, he was both the guide and the follower.

The next day Dr. Kalam reached Thumba. Though emotionally broken, he was committed to complete the unfinished work.

When he reached Thumba the director of Vikram Sarabhai Space Centre Dr. Brahmaprakash informed him that the veteran German rocket scientist Dr. Werner Van Braun was to visit India. Dr. Brown was recognized as among eminent scientists. Wernher Magnus Maximilian, Freiherr von Braun was a German (and later

American) aerospace engineerand space architect credited with inventing the V-2 Rocket and the Saturn-V, for Nazi Germany and the United States, respectively. He was one of the leading figures in the development of rocket technology in Nazi Germany, where he was also a member of the Nazi Party and the SS. Following the war he moved to the United States, where he developed the rockets that launched America's first space satellite and first series of moon missions. NASA has called him the "Father of Rocket Science".

Dr. Braun's visit to India was a very important event as his other achievements in the field of rocket science was the rocket 'Saturn' which had carried the first American to the moon. These important achievements had made him famous not only in the U.S.A. but throughout the world.

Indian rocket scientists were very enthusiastic about the visit of this important personality to India. Dr. Kalam was assigned the duty of escorting him from the Chennai airport to Thumba.

Talking about this journey Dr. Kalam says that he had not even imagined that Dr. Brown would be so polite. He had ability to accept and encourage the new scientists. When Dr. Kalam told him about the ratio and the diameter of the SLV, he cautioned and told Dr. Kalam, "This can cause aero electric problem."

Finally Dr. Braun's words proved to be true.

In 1979 a team of six members was busy in preparing transformation of flight. Only fifteen minutes earlier they came to know that one of the twelve valves had got some defect. Before any action could be taken on the testing spot, the tank of the nitric acid burst. Some members got serious burns when this acid fell on them. They were soon hospitalized. This failure shocked Dr. Kalam and his teammates, but they did not give up and continued with the project.

After the situation returned to normal the first practical flight of SLV was made on the 10th of August 1979 at 7:58 a.m. It was launched from Sriharikota. The first step of this launch was successful. It was to be converted into the 2nd phase when suddenly it was out of control. The flight stopped after 317 seconds and the SLV fell into the ocean about 525 km away from Sriharikota.

This raised questions on the capability of rocket science and the scientists in the country. Dr. Kalam and his colleagues had failed this time also. Dr. Kalam was more disappointed with these frequent failures. During this distress and misery Dr. Brahmaprakash consoled him and said that it was not only his failure but all those who were with him during the operation. Saying this he consoled all those who were working with him on the SLV project.

Now, it was time to analyse the reasons of failure. During the probe the scientists found that the nitric acid that worked as the oxidizer had flown out of the system and one of the valves had remained open. Dr. Kalam took all the responsibility of the failure and said, "It was my responsibility to check the leakage of the acid in the final moments, hence, I am the culprit." This statement of Dr. Kalam brought complete silence in the hall.

Two months later in the first week of November 1979, Dr. Brahmaprakash got retired. Only after nine months of his retirement the second launch of SLV was made on 18th July 1980 at 8.03 a.m. from the Sriharikota range. Dr. Kalam was very cautious this time. It was the first successful Indian rocket launch. The rocket was stabilised in the lower orbit of the earth only after two minutes of the launch. Dr. Kalam reported to all the stations after this success, "All the sections have completed the requirements of the expedition."

The engine of the fourth phase also activated to set up the satellite in the orbit. This success made the whole nation happy. This brought India in the category of some selected nations which were able to launch a rocket on its own. The Indian Parliament welcomed it with great pleasure. The erstwhile Prime-Minister Mrs. Indira Gandhi, congratulated all the scientists and co-workers. Not only India had taken a step forward to explore space, but also it was the beginning of the national progress in a new field and fulfilment of the nation's dreams.

   Pride of the Nation: Dr. A.P.J. Abdul Kalam

The next day the Parliamentary Committee of Science and Technology met in the annexe of parliament. The Prime Minister told the members about the success of SLV-3 and praised Dr. Kalam's contribution.

Now, since the SLV-3 project was completed, Dr. Kalam moved out from it. It was time to reorganize the accomplishments of VSSC after the successful completion of SLV-3. Ved Prakesh Sandlas was appointed the director of the SLV-3 project after Dr. Kalam.

The next goal of this project was to explore a number of possibilities. To strengthen SLV technologically, to increase the payload capacity and making of PSLV to reach the 9 km. orbit were planned. These important missions required Dr. Kalam's contribution. Therefore he was assigned the work of Director of Aerospace Dynamics & Design Group. Dr. Kalam prepared the analysis of the future projects and started comparative studies of different rocket launchers and use of missiles in the world. His intensive studies resulted into the conclusion that SLV-3 rocket system could establish the satellite upto a height of 4,000km. The next launch of SLV3 was done on 31st of May, 1981 in the name of SLV-3D. This was also a successful launch. It was the first occasion for Dr. Kalam when he watched the launch from the visitor's gallery and not from inside the control room.

Honour of Padma Bhushan

26th of January, 1981 added one feather in Dr Kalam's cap, for being   awarded with Padma Bhushan. This honour not only pleased Dr. Kalam, but the whole aeronautical group was rejoiced. Dr. Kalam says, "I felt very happy for the first time as if I was in the lap of my mother and my father is celebrating with joy. My brother-in-law is dancing with joy among my village folks and my sister is busy preparing sweets. Sri Lakshman Shastri is blessing me and I am the centre of attraction in the crowd of Father Solomon, Prof. Sarabhai and other well-wishers."

Dr. Kalam says, "My life is like nature. To achieve anything I have never tried to become cruel."

By then Dr. Kalam's name was among the scientists who have achieved tremendous success. This achievement had made his senior colleagues jealous of him and he wanted to eradicate this. By chance he was invited by 'High Altitude Laboratory' at Dehradun to deliver a speech on SLV-3. Dr. Kalam delivered a long speech on SLV-3 there under the chairmanship of famous atomic scientist, Prof. Ramanna who was an advisor to Defence Minister. Prof. Ramanna invited Dr. Kalam for tea after the speech and without any formality offered him the responsibilities of DRDO (Defence Research and Development Organisation).

Those days the project on testing atom bomb was in progress. DRDO required an experienced personality who could successfully lead the project in Pokharan. Dr. Kalam accepted the proposal with happiness. Prof. Ramanna asked him to see Prof. Dhawan so that he could arrange his transfer from ISRO to DRDO.

Quite a few months were spent on the departmental proceedings. DRDO was very keen on getting Dr. Kalam's services whereas ISRO did not want to leave him. Both ISRO and DRDO kept on discussing the issue for long.

Lastly on 1st June, 1982 Dr. Kalam joined DRDL (Defence Research and Development Laboratory) as its Director. Five Schemes and many large-scale and small-scale projects of manufacturing were under process in DRDL. Meanwhile the Anna University of Chennai honoured him with the honorary degree of 'Doctor of Science'. This degree recognized his contribution in the field of Rocket Engineering.

When he started looking into the responsibility of DRDL, he found lack of zeal in the scientists working there because many projects were abandoned or left half-done due to adverse government policies. One of these was a very important project, the 'Devil Missile Project'.

Working here Dr. Kalam could sense the pain of the world of scientists due to which scientists lacked in zeal and confidence. He

   Pride of the Nation: Dr. A.P.J. Abdul Kalam

started thinking on the lines of how to enhance the morale of the talented scientists.

Tactical Vehicle Project

Incidentally the chief of naval forces, Admiral A.S. Dawson visited the DRDL. Dr. Kalam found it to be a good opportunity. He put the file of his future projects before the Admiral. 'The Tactical Core Vehicle Project' was one among them. It had been stopped long time ago. This project was about two types of missile firing: One was about firing from land to air and the other was about firing missiles from air to land.

Dr. Kalam explained this project to the Admiral in detail and at the same time he put stress on the significant use of missile during wars on the sea. Finally Admiral Dawson liked this project. The scientists working in the laboratory were also encouraged to learn that their new director was concentrating on resuming these useful projects.

The work on the project of land-to-land missile started in DRDL. This filled the scientists of the organization with zeal. Seeing the good results Dr. Kalam reviewed different sub-systems and decided to induct experienced scientists and engineers from different institutions of the country to the DRDL. He called many a scientist from Indian Institute of Science, Indian Institute of Technology and Tata Institute of Fundamental Research. This resulted in the creation of a talent pool in DRDL.

Now it was essential to promote the research and development works in DRDL. Dr. Kalam has mentioned, "In my life I have given importance to openness of thoughts regarding scientific researches and works. I have always avoided gossiping in closed rooms and secret managements as it not only creates difference of opinions in the colleagues but also it disrupts validity."

Hence, to encourage his colleagues, he constituted a forum of senior scientists so that collective discussions could be held on matters pertaining to projects. In this way he framed a Missile Technology Committee. This committee was a beginning of a system in which the Management worked jointly.

Another committee was formed for the production of indigenous missile and Dr. Kalam was made its chairman. Apart from Dr. Kalam, Z.P. Marshall, the chief of Bharat Dynamics Limited, Hyderabad, N. R. Iyer, K.S. Venkatraman and A.K. Kapoor were included in the committee. Dr. Kalam prepared a detailed document and budget to present his projects before the Cabinet Committee. The budget showed an estimated expenditure of Rs. 90 crore during the next 12 years.

In this budget Dr. Kalam had mentioned the development and production of two types of missiles—one was a quick firing at lower height missile and the other was land to land medium distance missile. Dr. Kalam and his colleagues had not hoped that the government would sanction the project.

R. Venkatraman was the Defence Minister then and this proposal was sent to the cabinet. All the three Service chiefs, General Krishna Rao, Air Chief Marshal Dil Bagh Singh and Admiral Dawson, were also in the meeting of the Budget Committee. Everybody was anxiously waiting for the sanction of the budget. Dr. Kalam was worried about the amount of money to be sanctioned. If the committee sanctioned less money, how would he complete the project?

The meeting continued for several hours. When the meeting was over, the Defence Minister told Dr. Kalam to see him in the evening and got up.

In the evening when Dr. Kalam and his colleagues met the Minister they were very happy to know that Rs. 388 crore was sanctioned for their project.

Flight from 'Prithvi' to 'Agni'

There was no chance of any obstacle in the way of the development programmes now. The Integrated Guided Missile Development Programme (IGMDP) was started in a jiffy. The proposed projects were named 'Prithvi', 'Trishul', 'Nag', 'Agni' and 'Akash'.

Prithvi could be used at any point in the range of 250 km of distance. This was a land-to-land missile. This is why it was named Prithvi and the tactical core vehicle was named 'Trishul' (the missile of Lord Shiva). The land-to-air project was started with the name 'Nag'. The project of 'Agni' missile was also started simultaneously.

Some difficulties came in the way when Prithvi project was started in 1983. Some important metals like navigational sensors, tankage etc necessary for the project were not available in our country. These were procured by indigenous means. Regular new experiments were being conducted. This missile influenced the whole world with its new software and qualities. The success of this missile resulted in the developing of new generation of scientists.

Missiles Produced/Directed by Dr. Kalam

Prithvi: This missile can hit at any point within a range of 250 km. of distance. It can carry explosives upto 125 kg. It has three Issues:

Name	Strike capacity/weight	Issues
Prithvi-1	150 km/100 kg payload	Land Force
Prithvi-2	250 km/500 kg. payload	Air Force
Prithvi-3	350 km/500 kg payload	Naval Force

Trishul: This missile can strike land-to-air and land-to- land upto 15 km. of distance.

Akash: This is land-to-land missile with strike capacity of 25 km. It can carry a payload upto 55 kg.

Nag: This missile is antagonistic to tanks. Its strike capacity is about 15 km. It was tested successfully on 4th of December in the Chandipur range in Orissa.

Agni: The preparation of this missile is, in fact, Dr. Kalam's dream coming true. Many different tests of this missile have taken place—Agni-1, Agni-2, Agni-3 etc. These proved worthy on the scale of science. It is a reliable land-to-land missile and its strike capacity is even more than 1500 km. It can carry a payload of about 1000 kg. This missile also has three issues:

Name	Strike capacity	Payload capacity
Agni-1	600-750	500 kg.
Agni-2	2000-2500	1000 kg.
Agni-3	3000+	1000 kg.

The former Indian President Dr. A. P. J. Abdul Kalam said:

"Many individuals with myopic vision questioned the relevance of space activities in a newly independent nation, which was finding it difficult to feed its population. Their vision was clear if Indians were to play meaningful role in the community of nations, they must be second to none in the application of advanced technologies to their real-life problems. They had no intention of using it as a means of displaying our might."

History of the Missiles

Dr. Kalam believed that missiles were first invented in ancient India. In the ancient times they were called 'Astra' which we now call a missile. We still find the names of 'Narayan Astra', 'Agneyastra', 'Brahmastra', 'Varunastra' etc. in our mythological stories.

There is a painting hanging in NASA, the greatest name in the world of space research in which the soldiers of Tipu Sultan are shown fighting against the British army with rockets. This painting keeps Tipu Sultan's dreams in the 18th century alive. This painting proves that Tipu Sultan had made such rockets which could be used in face-to-face battle. The present improved rockets are only modifications of that rocket. Tipu Sultan was killed in 1799. the British army had recovered 700 such rockets from him. Nine hundred sub-systems of rockets were also found. Those rockets were taken to Britain. The work on rocket science research gained momentum.

Russia in 1903, America in 1914 and Germany in 1923 gave new directions to the world of rocket science. Dr. Werner Van Braun made short distance V-2 missiles in Nazi Germany. These were used in the Second World War. After the war, both the Americans and the Russians took the German rocket technique and the German engineers to their countries. After this the researches on missiles and other weapons became a continuous process in these countries.

The credit of starting work on rocket science in India goes to our first Prime Minister, Pandit Jawahar Lal Nehru. When India got free from the cruel clutches of the British, the economic condition of the country was poor. In spite of this, Pandit Nehru took an initiative in space program after considering the importance of rocket science. Prof. Sarabhai was always with him in this endeavor.

Operation Shakti

Dr. Kalam proved the fact, "Anything can be achieved with the help of modesty and hard labour." He always worked with determined dedication and always got positive results. Dr. Kalam spent most of his life in the research wing of the Defence Ministry. His creativity and zeal made him a legend.

He first joined DRDO (Defence Research and Development Organisation) as a scientist. Later he was promoted to the post of Director and then to the post of Director General. In the intervening period he made a very important contribution to ISRO, the prominent institute of space research. Many talented scientists worked under his leadership in several laboratories.

His research and new experiments not only made him successful and a top ranking scientist, it also laid a strong foundation to build modern India. Dr. Kalam's achievements emanate from his nobility, modesty and devotion which were amply evident even during his initial "Hovercraft" days.

The Hovercraft

This craft could fly in air and float on water as well. It had been planned much earlier to make a craft which should be wingless, light in weight and studded with a swift machine. Dr. Kalam made a thorough study of the technical differences between a hovercraft and an aircraft. He believed that a man must work to understand any project. Once he does this, it is not impossible to complete it.

The work of manufacturing a hovercraft was in process since the decade of 1960. Dr. Kalam says, "The machinery that I was using in the manufacture of the craft was different from what was

            Pride of the Nation: Dr. A.P.J. Abdul Kalam

planned and hence, on many occasions I had to bear the wrath of the senior colleagues."

Most of the senior colleagues of the team believed that the young Kalam would not be able to manufacture the craft with his unconventional ways of a novice. Dr. Kalam paid no attention to the criticism and continued to work. He kept on working on the structure of the craft using new methods and also encouraged his colleagues to do similarly.

Finally, the very important day arrived when the craft was ready. It was named 'Nandi'—the carriage of Lord Shiva. The hovercraft weighing 550 kilos was standing on the air cushion, ready to fly. Everybody was astonished to see the spherical piece of machine. Dr. Kalam told his bewildered colleagues. "Please don't look at it with astonishment. It is a flying machine, board it and fly in the air." The then Defence Minister, Mr. V.K. Krishna Menon, himself enjoyed its first flight ignoring all safety norms. Mr. Menon sanctioned its production through his ministry but unfortunately he had to resign from his post and the project of 'Nandi' was abandoned.

Composite Structure

Dr. Kalam prepared such a composite structure for Roto motor casing that would not break easily. Earlier it was made of wood, iron or some other metal which was always in danger of breaking and at the same time they were heavier also. They stopped working at high temperature.

Dr. Kalam made a thorough study to make an improved composite. He had chosen the filament fibre glass as an alternative for composite structure when he was working in ISRO. Apart from this he had also developed high energy composite propellant, phenomenon-based ignition system and the jet system. He established a Fibre Reinforced Plastic Division in Thiruvananthapuram and prepared the composite mixing the fibres of plastic and jute. The pressure machine of higher technique was also prepared with the help of this very composition. During these experiments only the rocket motor lids were developed to be used in the third and fourth chambers of SLV. Earlier, they were made of glass which was not safe.

SLV (Satellite Launch Vehicle)

Dr. Kalam's first major success was establishing a satellite in the space. It was also the first important achievement for ISRO. Dr. Kalam was in search of some such technique which could fire the satellites into the space. For this one such rocket motor was to be developed which could work successfully in all the four chambers of the vehicle. Also one such instrument was required which could have full control over the vehicle. Hence, about 300 big and small machineries were manufactured from many metals and composites. Dr. Kalam won laurels all over the world for this achievement and he was also honoured with 'Padma Bhushan'.

Subsequently, he was honored with the highest civil decoration 'Bharat Ratna' in 1997.

Integrated Program

Integrated Program means manufacturing missile under a whole program in India. After an detailed and serious discussions , the Defence Minister Mr. R. Venkatraman assigned this responsibility to Dr. Kalam. Five missiles—Trishul, Prithvi, Akash, Nag and Agni—were proposed to be designed under this project.

Brahmos: This missile has been named taking 'Brahma' from the Brahmaputra river in India and 'Mos' from the Moskva river in Russia. Dr. Kalam and his team from India and Russia worked jointly on this project. The project on this supersonic anti-ship cruise missile has already been completed now and it has been included in the Artillery Batallion of Indian Army. Dr. Kalam had to face many difficulties in getting this joint venture sanctioned. Brahmos is a supersonic cruise missile which can be used on the sea, under the sea and also in the air. It is designed for use on the ships.

Operation 'Shakti': India tested the first atomic weapon on 18th May 1974 from Pokhran in the Thar Desert, about 153 km away from the Pakistan border. It was tested underground and was successful. Thus India is the seventh nation joining atomic powers of the world after U.S.A., Britain, Russia, France, Canada and China. After this, India has conducted 3 nuclear tests on 11th May and 2 tests on 13th May 1998 from Pokhran .

Establishing itself as a nuclear power in the world, Government of India constituted the Nuclear Command Authority for this. A political council and a working committee would be at the head of this authority. The Prime Minister would be the head of the political council, and the army could use nuclear weapons against the enemies only after the approval by this council. The National Security Council would be the head of the working committee. The government has also constituted a separate strategic force command having all the three wings of the army as its constituents to administer the nuclear weapons. The two operational missile groups of the land force have been brought under strategic force command.

Dr. Kalam's Contribution to the Military Forces

Our country will never forget. Dr. Abdul Kalam's services to the army. May be the missiles developed by Dr. Kalam are not the need of the present age, but their induction was very important in order to bring India among the leading developed nations of the world. The following is the list of modem resources contributing in the security of the nation:

Land Force: The Indian army is studded with all modern weapons. The Vijayant tank made in Awadi is a big asset of the country. Its speed is 56 km/hr. It was very successfully used in the Indo-Pak war in 1971. The foreign tanks that India has are (1) AMX-13 (France), (2) Centurian (Britain), (3) P.T. 76, (4) T-5, (5) T-55 and (6) T-90 (Russia).

Indian Naval Force: The Indian Naval Force is equipped with modern warships. INS Virat is an aircraft Carrier ship. INS Mysore is an 8000 tons cruiser. INS Cora warship was launched on the 10th of August 1998 The indigenous missile launcher ship INS Prabal was given to the Indian Naval Force in Bombay on 11th April, 2002. It should be noted that this ship was launched on 28th September, 2000. The survey ship, INS Survekshak, was given to the Indian naval Force on 14th January, 2002. Naval ship, INS Ghariyal was included in the Eastern Range of the India Navy on 14th February, 1997. This Naval ship of the Landing Ship Tank class, is capable of carrying the Arjun tank alongwith other indigenous tanks. INS 'Prahar' was included in the India Naval Force on 1st March, 1997. The kilo class submarine INS Sindhushastra studded with anti-ship club missiles was included in the Indian Naval Force on 19th July, 2000 in a celebration in Saint Petersberg (Russia). INS Kaveri is with the Indian Naval Force which is a submarine obtained from the Soviet Union.

Frigates: INS Trishul and Talwar are anti-sub-marine frigates. Brahmaputra, Vyas and Betwa are anti-aircraft frigates. Anti-sub-marine ship Nilgiri has been manufactured in the Mazagaon Dock. 'Himgiri', 'Udaigiri' and 'Dunagiri' are also frigate ships. Ferry-destroyers INS 'Vidyut' and 'Missile' are also launched. INS 'Aditya' (Tankship) and INS 'Brahmaputra' (Guided Missile Frigate) have also been included in the India Naval Force.

Destroyers: INS 'Ranjit', 'Rana', 'Rajput', 'Ganga', 'Godawari', 'Gomah' and 'Ranveer' are destructive ships.

Air Force: Indian Air Force is using a variety of aircrafts which are:

Helicopters: M.I.-8, M.I.-17, M.I.-25, M.I.-26, M.I.-35 Cheetah, Chetak etc.

Training Crafts: H.P.T.-32, H.J.T.-16 (Kiran), Iskara, H.S.- 748.

Fighters and Bombers: Ajeet, MIG-21, MIG-23, MIG-29, Jaguar, Miraj-2000, Sukhoi-30 etc. Jaguar has replaced the old bomber Canberra.

Pilotless Aircrafts: India has manufactured 'Nishant' which is a pilotless aircraft. It was successfully tested on 26th April, 2000 at Chandipur Testing Range in Orissa. Another pilotless aircraft 'Lakshya' was also successfully tested from Chandipur, Orissa

            Pride of the Nation: Dr. A.P.J. Abdul Kalam

on 2nd November 2000. 'Lakshya' was again tested successfully second time in March 2002.

Carriage Aircrafts: A.N.-32, I.L.-14, Cairibu, T.U.-124,1- 76, H-.S.-748, Dornear-228 etc.

Missiles: India has successfully tested many indigenous missiles in the recent years. Most of them have been handed over to the Indian military. These missiles are 'Prithvi' and 'Agni' series (land-to-land), Trishul' and 'Akash' (land-to-air) and 'Nag' (anti-tank missiles). India has successfully tested 'Dhanush' the Naval mode of the 'Prithvi' missile on 11th April, 2000 from the Chandipur Centre coast through INS 'Samudra'. One ultra-modern supersonic cruise missile, 'Brahmos' was tested successfully from Chandipur, Orissa on 12th June, 2001 by a combination of Indian and Russian scientists. It was again successfully tested on 28th April 2002 from the same Chandipur centre.

Reverberation of Pokhran

Dr. Homi Jehangir Bhabha believed that atoms and molecules are in the nature from the very ancient times. India would prove her worth of being counted among the best class nations of the world with the help of the rebirth of atoms.

USA, the established world power, has done a number of nuclear tests. The Americans killed millions of people by dropping atom bombs on Hiroshima of Japan during the 2nd World War. USA has many nuclear weapons even today. America always has the desire that no other nation of the world should compete with it in the matter of nuclear weapons. This is why the Pokharan nuclear test by India in 1998 was criticized and it made comments on the Pokhran blast followed by enforcing economic and trade sanctions on India.

It should be noted that a campaign to destroy nuclear weapons is being pursued on the international level but the world peace proposal is not making progress. Every country has the right to keep itself ready for its protection. Keeping this in view the then Prime Minister, Mrs. Indira Gandhi, had permitted the Pokhran Nuclear Test in 1974. She had decided to keep the nuclear weapon program a continuous process ignoring the worldwide criticism, but unfortunately she was assassinated in 1984 and the project was abandoned for long.

After this during the tenure of the then Prime Minister Mr. Narasimha Rao the project took a few steps forward but again India had to keep quiet due to opposing attitude of the countries who were called nuclear powers then.

Finally in 1998 India conducted Pokhran-2 test and it was a success. The credit of this achievement goes to Prime Minister, Mr. A.B. Vajpayee, who showed his courage to the world. Dr. Kalam is also given the credit as he contributed a lot to make it a success.

The nuclear test-2 was conducted under the supervision of Dr. Kalam and Dr. R. Chidambaram, the President of Atomic Energy Commission, with the support of the Department of Atomic Energy and DRDO.

Atomic Policy

It is a big question that the proposal of 'Earth without a nuclear weapon' comes from those countries which have a good store of nuclear weapons. The use of only 10% of the reserved store can destroy the whole earth in a few seconds. What the man has on earth as a fruit of his very hard labour for millions of years can be destroyed within moments. It is a matter of worldwide criticism that the countries who preach disarmament of nuclear weapons themselves have a large stock of atomic arsenal which should essentially be controlled. It is a big irony that those nations do not want to destroy their nuclear weapons, but preach the others not to take up atomic programmes. If they really want world peace, they must destroy their own stock of destructive nuclear weapons.

The statement of the then Foreign Minister Mr. Jaswant Singh in this connection is praiseworthy. He said, "India will sign the CTBT only when it is recognised as an atomic power of the world." If we are a nuclear power, why should we accept that we don't have any nuclear weapon?

The Pokhran-2 test has established that India is one of the nuclear powers of the world. It should be mentioned here that India had sketched its atomic policy only after the 1974 Pokhran Nuclear Test. Hence it can't be denied that India has sufficient stock of nuclear energy and the credit for this goes to Dr. Homi Jahangir Bhabha and Dr. A.P.J. Abdul Kalam.

Dr. Kalam as President of India

Dr. Kalam became President of India on 25th of July 2002. He is the first President who is not only an avid philosopher and spiritualist, but also is a great nuclear scientist and a guide for the new generation scientists. His determination and the capacity to carry a project to its ultimate goal are the basis for people to call him the 'missile-man'.

The journey of Dr. Kalam's life till today has seen many odds. He was very keen on studying during his childhood. Though he was born in a poor family, his father wanted him to study and thereby earn a name for the nation. Dr. Kalam says that his father's daily routine started with the first 'Namaz' at 4 in the morning. After that he tried to tell Dr. Kalam about the basic truths. He used to tell Abdul Kalam that a man should not run away from troubles and distress but should try to find out its reasons.

This divine statement of his father guided the simple Abdul Kalam to become an engineer then a missile-man and finally to President Abdul Kalam.

Napoleon Bonaparte said, "He, who is afraid of failure, must fail." Dr. Kalam was always sure of his win and success.

It won't be wrong if we call Dr. A.P.J. Abdul Kalam an extraordinary President of India. It was not only the unconventional hair style, or dislike for the formal dress and the luxury and the pomp and show, he was is known for his simplicity and emotive energy. Perhaps this is the reason why the children of the country liked him to be a simple President, different from the others.

The President is provided with domestic help.. But Dr. Kalam never accepted any such help. He liked to do most of the work himself. He liked plain and vegetarian food. He climbed up the stairs running. He liked children as they are the future generation of the nation. Children called him, 'Chacha Kalam' or 'Kalam Uncle'. Dr. Kalam had the heartfelt desire to elevate India to the category of developed nations.

One of his helps speaks endearingly, "He has measured the whole 330 acres of the 'Rashtrapati Bhawan' on foot." There is no doubt that Dr. Kalam had not only become the President of the country but of the people also. His working style did not change even after becoming the President. Within a year's time he visited almost all important nations. He got up very early and took a morning walk in open air regularly. He performed prayers and yoga daily. Reading books on science, economics and religion was his habit. He bowed down with equal reverence in a temple, a mosque and a church. He had equal liking for the Holy Quran, Srimad Bhagwadgita and the Bible. He was crowned with 'Kanchi Parmacharya Samman' in 1997 despite his belonging to a different faith.

He liked meeting children. He not only went to their schools to meet them, but also called them to the 'Rashtrapati Bhawan'. His life style was purely radical. On the one hand he disliked hypocrisy and ostentation and on the other hand he did not show anger.

Dr. Kalam was highly praised throughout the country for his journey to Gujarat. When he was talking to the victims of the rioting, it appeared that the President was a friend, a healer, a provider and a good adviser.

During his visit to Gujarat neither he questioned any government official publicly nor he contacted any political party. But when he was advising the Gujarat Government to eradicate the problems of the riot victims, his style was quite political. This visit of Dr. Kalam touched the people's hearts. After this he visited Mahatma Gandhi's birth place, Porbandar. Though this visit of his provided the political parties opportunity of discussions, some called it a projected visit; others called it an unwanted intervention.

The Ex-President Dr. R. Venkatraman claimed this visit to be in the welfare of public. He even told that a President could not live like a captive of the Rashtrapati Bhawan. He must be worried about the mishaps in the country.

Neither Dr. Kalam is a politician nor did he like the mean activities of politics. He was a popular scientist of the country. He did not have any future political aims. On the whole we can say that his dutifulness to the nation proved that he was not swayed by splendour and the customs of his post, but to his sense of responsibilities such that no glamour could deter him.

He was such a President who looked into any affair with the eyes of a modern scientist. This is why he started working in the direction of setting up a paperless office as soon as he took up the charge. As a scientist and teacher he still had his students in contact. The Anna University of Chennai had provided him with the facility of Video conferencing for his lectures. For this purpose only he has got the internet connection at the Raisina Hill—the Rashtrapati Bhawan — converted in 2 megabyte per second from 56 kilobytes per second. India was graced with a President who traveled in the Cyberspace.

Kalam and Vajpayee: Similarities

There are many personality related similarities between the President Dr. Abdul Kalam and the Prime Minister Mr. Atal Behari Vajpayee. These are:

- Both were unmarried. Once Dr. Kalam joked to one of his friends: "Had I been married, I won't have achieved even half of what I have now." His elder brother once fixed his marriage, but he could not reach timely and gradually he became overaged for marriage.

- None of the two has any near-relatives.

- Both have the same nature and simplicity.

- Both are the examples of honesty and tolerance.

- Both Kalam and Vajpayee were attached to some magazines in the early life. The difference was that Vajpayee used to write and edit whereas Kalam used to sell newspapers in Rameshwaram. Both of them have composed poems.

- Most importantly, none of the two likes recommendations.

- Both of them avoid heavy expenses on them and are determined to cut them short.

Feeling the Pulse of India

Dr. Kalam was an atomic scientist who is called the 'Father of Atom Bomb' in India after the Pokhran atomic explosion. He won many awards and praise for his contributions to science. Dr. Kalam who has dreamt of India as a strong nation after taking up the charge of the President of India thought that dreams convert into thoughts and the thoughts come to us as our works and goals. Hence it is clear, "If there are no dreams, there won't be any thoughts and ultimately we won't have any work or goals."

Dr. Kalam's giving importance to power was an act of laying the foundation stone of a strong nation. He believed that power only respects power. After he became the President he had a dream of making India a fully developed nation by 2020. His vision portrayed the reformed India. In his imagination, Dr. Kalam has envisioned all those factors which would help us to make India a strong nation.

The projects on agriculture, industry, trade, education, health, security and commerce are included in his future course of action. For the execution of these projects Dr. Kalam has invoked all the intelligentsia, specialists, scientists, social reform organisations, the administration and journalists of India with one string.

After he became the President, he not only discussed with officers, scientists and engineers, but also visited schools and colleges to talk to the children about reforms and awareness. He believed that only an inquisitive person can become a scientist and children only have the most inquisitive brain. Children always try to know and understand new things. In fact the first scientist of the world might have been a child.

According to Dr. Kalam we should follow Gandhiji's thoughts which he had spread among the people of the country. They are 'Wealth can not be earned without labour'; 'Joy cannot be felt without an inner self;' 'Knowledge can't be gained without a good character'; 'No trade can be successful without moral values'. Similarly, Dr. Kalam said that politics cannot be successful without religion, principles and sacrifice.

Dr. Kalam always followed these principles. He believed that if after the greatest disaster during the Second World War Japan could revive just within 20 years and could leave America and Germany behind in science and technology, why can't India do so? All that was needed was a burning desire to fix the goal and act with full force to achieve it.

     Pride of the Nation: Dr. A.P.J. Abdul Kalam

The aim of Dr. Kalam was to build a strong India. He had fixed a mission for which the time limit is 2020. He founded a trust by the name 'Developed India Foundation' purely with his seed money. He had a plan of working independently with the help of this trust. Dr. Kalam's becoming President of India was an important step in this direction.

It is needless to say that the image of Dr. Kalam as the 11th President of India is the index of his culture. He considered himself as an integral part of the. He was aware of his responsibilities. He was a winner who always concentrated on his potential strengths and worked on his weaknesses. This is the reason why Dr. Kalam is seen as an icon of Indianness. All the religions in India believed that Dr. Kalam was a strong pillar secular thought in the country.

Other than these Dr. Kalam was a perfect ideal for those who believed that knowledge is incomplete without foreign education. Dr. Kalam never went abroad for his education. He completed his education in Tamil Nadu itself.

Straight Talk

Dr. Kalam's memory power was fresh even after eight decades of life. He was still concerned about the development of the country's science and technology. He expressed his views on knowledge and science before the youth or the young generation in such a way that his words became an inspiration for them. He inspired people to make their dreams by sincerity and hard work.

Dr. Kalam had met with lakhs of children and inspired them. One cannot notice any difference in his life-style as a scientist before becoming the President and the later life-style as a President. He liked talking on social matters. One saw gathering of teachers, scientists, doctors, social reformers, engineers and farmers and of course the school-children surrounding him. He worked for 18-20 hours even in his old age. On an average he met 15-20 people every day, replied to hundreds of e-mails, sent autographs to many of his fans as a routine. Other than these he relentlessly pursued his dream of 2020.

A child asked him on the occasion of the annual day celebration of Saint Mary School, Tamil Nadu why he advised people to see dreams. He replied, "Dreams become thoughts and these are the thoughts which convert into our works and goals. If there are no dreams, there won't be any revolutionary thoughts."

Another student asked, "Who would have been the first scientist?" This question plunged Dr. Kalam into deep thought. After pondering for a while he replied, "I think, it would have been a child." The whole hall applauded him with claps.

He came in contact with school children during the convocation of Tezpur University, Assam. A child asked him such a question related to politics. The question was, "Why isn't the water of the overflowing Brahmaputra River carried to states like Rajasthan and Tamil Nadu where water is scarce?" Dr. Kalam sensed that the question was difficult. He admitted that the question was so difficult that even the Prime Minister won't be able to answer it. Since it was very difficult for him to convince children on this issue he replied that states own the rivers and they kept on quarrelling on the issue due to political interference.

In fact, people who divide land don't consider that air and water cannot be divided. He satisfied the children by saying, "It is expected in the 'Vision 2020' that after growing up you execute the work of joining all the rivers. When all the rivers are joined together, there won't be any clashes for water." Some children claimed that big leaders don't visit their state. Dr. Kalam consoled those children saying that he would talk to the Prime Minister when he is back to Delhi.

It is needless to mention that the travelogue of Dr. Abdul Kalam not only touches the different aspects, but also reveals the unsaid sentiments. The innocent and impartial thoughts of the children and their curiosity can only make a strong India. These facts expose the evils of our society and country and at the same time sketch the developing manifestation.

Undoubtedly, Dr. Kalam's personality, character and philosophy of life did not change even after he became the President of India. The thoughts of this scientist and philosopher President appeared to be futuristic and filled with optimism. This is why a person standing before him felt refreshed and even a simple sentence from his mouth became an epoch- making statement.

When he visited Jharkhand after it had gained statehood, children from Ramakrishna High School, Bokaro surrounded him. One of them asked, "Sir, Jharkhand is surrounded by greenery from all around. It has hills, dense forests and springs. But Rajasthan is a fallow land. Why so?"

Though from the point of view of science, the answer to this question was complicated, Dr. Kalam gave a very balanced answer, "Children! Do you know? Farming in Rajasthan was not so easy twenty years ago as it is now. How it happened? In fact a canal namely Indira Gandhi Canal was dug there which has made the land of Rajasthan fertile at many places. More development is on cards which you children will execute."

Some other child asked, "Sir, can your rocket (Agni Missile) reach America?" Dr. Kalam smiled and said, "America is our friend and Agni is the symbol of our might. We don't aim at showing our strength to any country but on protecting ourselves."

Similarly in Gujarat during a celebration an intelligent child asked Dr. Kalam, "Sir, who is our enemy?" Dr. Kalam said, "Your question is a very good one." He asked the other children over there to find its answer. He did so because he required a little time to make out its answer. Suddenly a young girl spoke out in a philosophical style," Poverty is our greatest enemy." Clearly there was a hidden meaning in this answer which echoed the unemployment in our country.

"Please tell me, whose weapons are stronger, India's or Pakistan's?" asked an argumentative child. Dr. Kalam told in order to convince him, "India is capable to make any type of nuclear weapon. We have all that we should have. Rickets or missiles, whatever we have are the strength of our nation. We should never forget that might only honours might and not the weakness. This might/strength means our military force and economic prosperity; it never means to show our might before other countries.

During his visits within the country Dr. Kalam was able to know that children of the present era are so inquisitive about our past and future that he wanted them to become the witness of the future. Clearly this type of questions from curious children can only help in building a strong and beautiful India.

He visited Cuttack on the invitation of Justice Rangnath Mishra.

Some youth asked him about his favourite books that developed his thoughts and views.

That time Dr. Kalam spoke of four books. The first one was, "Man, The Unknown" written by Nobel Prize holder Dr. Alexis Carrel. The author has mentioned in the book that - during any illness, the patient must be treated both physically and mentally. It is not certain that a patient can recover only using medicines. The nervous system of the body also plays a vital role in the recovery of a patient. He advised that all the medical students must read this book. The second was related to the 'action plan' of life. The third was "Lights From Many Lamps" by Lillian Watson . He said the fourth book that inspired him is "The Quran Sharif". He also said these four books helped him not only in testing a man but also makes him a good man.

Facts and not the logics are required to know the President Dr. A.P.J. Abdul Kalam. These facts are the memories of his life of struggle.

When he was invited by the Vice-Chancellor of the Gorakhpur University on the occasion of convocation, he accepted it gladly. He met with the teachers as well as the students and also discussed many important issues related to the development of the state.

In his address, the President requested U.P. to play the same role it had played for the country's development by leading the Indian Freedom Movement in 1857. He also talked about 'Vision 2020' and to double the rate of development he spoke of five factors from integrated work system to other sufficient resources.

He accorded utmost importance to agriculture and said, "We need to do a lot to encourage agriculture and the manure industry. We need to develop the electricity generation with new and modified techniques so that the supply of electricity is continuous." He claimed that education in India is also heading on the path of development after agriculture and electricity.

Country's development is possible through education, hence steps are afoot to make the maximum people of the nation literate.

The fall in the increasing rate of population in Kerala and Tamilnadu is only due to the literacy. We have to repeat it in other states also.

So far as information and technology is concerned Dr. Kalam believed that India is progressing perpetually. If atomic, space and military achievements are included, we can say that India is progressing uninterruptedly.

Apart from the above he also answered many questions from the students. This simple but great President expected three things from the students. First is to visit nearby villages and educate the villagers whenever they get a holiday. Second is to achieve the optimum in their academics. The third and the most important is that each and every person present there must plant at least five trees during his/her life time.

Replying a question he said that parents and the primary teachers are the best weapons for the war against corruption. Dr. Kalam did not forget to visit the grave of his favourite poet Kabir during this short visit of Gorakhpur. He reached Maghar without caring for the heavy rains and pitch darkness of night. There he listened to the couplets of Kabir from the saints.

This particular personality trait of Dr. Kalam distinguished him from the other Presidents. He wished that a complete picture of great India should emerge within his tenure so that we can be proud of becoming an example of progress, culture, friendliness and unity before the world. On the whole it can be said that Dr. Kalam, kept himself away from the splendour and hypocrisy of the Presidentship, emerged a head of the nation who broke away the old tradition, established his personal image and maintained its dignity.

India of the Future

According to Dr. A.P.J. Abdul Kalam the long term economic and security related aims based on different problems and analysis of their solutions formed the base for the structure of the future India. This helps in identifying different areas and initialising of the generation and use of knowledge.

In a literate society everybody must have the capacity to acquire knowledge within himself and everybody must get an opportunity to participate in the decision making process in order to give a proper shape to their capability. Special means are obtained from the basic structure of information and communication technology as these can transmit information to numerous people through different sources. It is necessary to implement the principle of knowledge for all so that it helps the formation of a literate society and knowledge economy. It is necessary to expand the access of conception so that mutual give-and-take and contribution of all can also be brought together.

Dr. Kalam wished that India should emerge as a great power systematically within a definite time-frame. For this we have to take forward some steps in the following way:

- India's emergence as a literate society: defining the concerned issues, determining their shapes and announcement of the public policies.

- To develop public awareness programmes.

- To prepare the annual progress report of the steps taken in order to make India a literate society.

- To develop a web-site to expose India's literate society.

- To include the illiterate part of the society in the efforts.

- To make a national stage to discuss publicly about the literate society of India.

- To find the issues of the literate society of India and eradicate them.

- Participation in the efforts in the direction of knowledge management by those who work for expressing Indian culture through information and communication structure.

- To contact different groups of the same interests and to promote such contacts.

- To promote all the activities helpful in obtaining these goals.

We know India is leading among the developing nations in respect of the data-base of knowledge. This is why developed nations like USA are looking towards India today in order to fulfil their need of their software. Thus we have all the means to make India a superpower of knowledge. India was a store of knowledge in the ancients times also.

Dr. Kalam expresses his hypothesis of India in 2020 in these words, "To make India a developed nation by 2020 or even before it is not merely a dream. It is also not only the speculation of a few Indians. Rather, it is such a mission related to the crores of Indians and we have to attain it."

Above 2000 years ago the great saint poet Thiruvalluvar had also put stress on the supremacy of knowledge. His message was like this, "Knowledge is that weapon which protects us from destruction. It is such a rampart within ourselves that saves us from enemies and from destruction."

Thus knowledge is a weapon of aggressiveness, defence and ambition. Our ancient sages, hermits and thinkers had known its importance thousands of years ago and had talked of knowledge-revolution. It happened at that time when none could have even thought of it in the world.

Development Dream in the Eyes of Dr. Kalam

The Bharat Darshan

Symbol of development	Present status	status by 2020
Population below poverty line	26	13
Rate of unemployment	7.3	6.8
Adult male literacy	6.8	9.6
Admission to primary schools	77.2	99.9
Percentage of GDP spent on education	3.2	4.9
Life expectation	64	69
Child deaths per 100 births	71	22.5
Malnutrition of children under 5 years of age 45	8	
Percentage of GDP spent on health	0.8	3.4
Consumption of energy per individual (equivalent to kilogram oil)	486.0	2002.0
Consumption of electricity KW per hour	384.0	2460.0
Telephones per thousand of population	34.0	203.0
Personal televisions per 1000	3.3	-
Scientists and engineers working for research and development (per lakh population)	149.0	590.0
Share percent in G.D.P.		
Agriculture	28.0	6,0
Industries	26.0	34.0
Services	46.0	60.0
Share of Direct Foreign investment in the formation of total capital	2.1	24.5

The Journey from
Science to Politics

Abdul Kalam's name was forwarded for the Presidentship with mutual agreement of members of BJP (Bhartiya Janta Party) and NDA. Later on all political parties including National Congress Party and Samajwadi Party supported the decision. On 18th July 2002, the eminent missile technologist was elected India's 11th President in a highly one-sided contest in which he bagged nearly 90 per cent vote value trouncing the Left-backed Colonel Lakshmi Sehgal in a preferential election system. India had seen ten presidents before Kalam. Three of them were highly skilled and great intellects. The other seven were true politicians.

Kalam knew little about politics when he first stepped into Rashtrapati Bhavan as the President of India. The Missile Man was now in a whole new world surrounded by the beauty of Mughal Garden that constantly inspired him to play melodious tunes on Veena. However, despite the striking transformation of a great scientist into a politician, Kalam was determined to tread on the path of justice.

Kalam's nomination as the President of India was not a coincidence. It was a well played political strategy wherein a lot of parties tried to pacify the aggression of Muslims after the Gujarat riots by recommending a name of a Muslim candidate. Political parties were quite impressed by a Muslim who read Bhagvad Geeta and practised vegetarianism. Congress and Samajwadi Parties could not oppose a Muslim as a candidate for Presidency especially one who made all attempts to make India a super power and a true patriot at heart.

Pride of the Nation: Dr. A.P.J. Abdul Kalam

While deciding for the swearing-in ceremony, Pramod Mahajan asked Kalam, "So what auspicious occassion would you like to choose for the ceremony?"

"As long as the solar system was in place, it's auspicious all the time." Kalam replied with a childlike smile on his face which was deadlier than all missiles.

The story behind Kalam's journey as a scientist to becoming a President is quite interesting. Kalam had mentioned this in his book 'The Turning Point'. Here is an excerpt from this book:

Dr. Kalam had written, "The morning of 10th June 2002 was like any other day in the beautiful environment of Anna University, where I had been working since December 2001. I had been enjoying my time in the large, tranquil campus, working with professors and inquisitive students on research projects and teaching. The authorized strength of my class was 60 students, but during every lecture, the classroom had more than 350 students and there was no way one could control the number of participants. My purpose was to understand the aspirations of the youth, to share my experiences from my many national missions and to evolve approaches for the application of technology for societal transformation through a specially designed course of ten lectures for postgraduate students. After a tiring day of giving lectures when I returned in the evening, the vice chancellor Anna University Kalanidhi informed that someone with a keen desire to contact me had called the office several times.

The phone was ringing as I reached my room. "Hello!" I said. "The Prime Minister wants to speak to you" was the answer on the other end.

As I waited to get connected to the Prime Minister, the then Chief Minister of Andra Pradesh Shri Chandra Babu Naidu called on my cell phone. As I was busy speaking to Naidu, the other call got connected to Shri Atal Bihari Vajpayeeji.

"How's academic life?" Atalji asked.

"Fantastic." I said.

Vajpayee continued, "We have some very important news for you. Just now, I am coming from a special meeting attended by leaders of all the coalition parties. We have decided unanimously that the nation needs you as its Rashtrapati. I have to announce this tonight. I would like to have your concurrence. I need only a 'Yes', not a 'No'." Vajpayee, I might mention, was heading the National Democratic Alliance (NDA), a coalition of almost two dozen parties, and it was not always easy getting unanimity.

I hadn't even had time to sit down after entering the room. Different images of the future appeared before me. One was that of being always surrounded by students and teachers. And the other, I was addressing the Parliament with a vision for the nation. A decision matrix was evolving in my mind. I said, "Vajpayeeji (as I normally addressed him), can you give me two hours' time to decide? It is also necessary that there must be a consensus among all political parties on my nomination as presidential candidate."

Vajpayee said, "After you agree, we will work for a consensus."

Over the next two hours, I must have made thirty telephone calls to my close friends. Among them were people in academia and friends in the civil services and in politics too. One view that came across was that I was enjoying an academic life, which is my passion and love, and I shouldn't disturb it. The second view was that this was an opportunity to put forth the India 2020 vision in front of the nation and Parliament, and that I must jump at it. Exactly after two hours, I was connected to the prime minister. I said, "Vajpayeeji, I consider this to be a very important mission and I would like to be an all-party candidate."

He said, "Yes, we will work for it, thank you."

The news travelled very fast indeed. Within 15 minutes, the news of my choice as presidential candidate was known throughout the country. Immediately, I was bombarded with an unmanageable number of telephone calls, my security was intensified and a large number of visitors gathered in my room.

The same day, Vajpayee consulted with Mrs. Sonia Gandhi, the

   Pride of the Nation: Dr. A.P.J. Abdul Kalam

opposition leader, about the choice of candidate. When Mrs Gandhi asked whether the NDA's choice was final, the prime minister responded in the affirmative. After due consultation with her party members and coalition partners, Mrs. Gandhi announced the support of the Indian National Congress (INC) to my candidature on 17th June 2002. I would have loved to get the support of the Left parties also but they decided to nominate their own candidate. As soon as I agreed to be a candidate for the presidency, a huge number of write-ups began to appear about me. Many questions were raised by the media. In essence, they were asking, how could a non-political person, particularly a scientist, become president of the nation?

On 18th June, at my first press conference after filing the nomination papers for my candidacy as president, journalists asked many questions regarding the Gujarat issue (the state had been racked by riots and there were concerns about how these were handled), Ayodhya (the Ram Janambhoomi issue was always in the news), the nuclear tests and about my plans in Rashtrapati Bhavan. I mentioned that India needed an educated political class with compassion as the cornerstone of decision making. On the Ayodhya issue, I mentioned that what the needed was education, economic development and respect for human beings. With economic development, societal differences would also reduce. I also pledged that I would maintain simplicity amidst the pomp and glory of Rashtrapati Bhavan. As president, on any complex issue, I would consult the country's leading constitutional experts. Decisions on issues such as President's Rule would be made on the basis of what people needed, rather than on what a few people wanted.

When I returned from Chennai to my flat in Asiad Village in Delhi on 10th July the preparations were in full swing. Pramod Mahajan of the Bhartiya Janata Party (BJP) was my election agent. I set up a camp office at the flat. It was not a large flat but it had a certain flexibility. I set up a visitors' room, the conference hall was made functional, and later even an electronic camp office was set up. All data was transmitted electronically. A letter was drafted for MPs – Lok Sabha as well as Rajya Sabha, so close to 800 in all – giving them my vision as president and asking them to vote for me. This was based on Mahajan's suggestion that I could send the letters without personally meeting the members of the electoral college from each state. As it turned out, I was declared elected on 18th July with a handsome margin. Kalam served as the 11th President of India, succeeding K. R. Narayanan. He won the 2002 presidential election with an electoral vote of 922,884, surpassing 107,366 votes won by Lakshmi Sahgal. He served from 25th July 2002 to 25th July 2007.

There were appointments with visitors, of whom there was a stream all through the day, and interviews with media besides my own correspondence and travel. I enjoyed interacting with children and when there was time I would listen to their responses on various issues. Flat No. 833 in Asiad Village became a beehive of activity. Just drawing up the guest list for the swearing-in ceremony on 25th July was an exercise in itself. The Central Hall of Parliament can only accommodate 1,000 people. Aside from the MPs, office-bearers of the two Houses, bureaucrats from the home and other ministries, and guests of the outgoing president, K.R. Narayanan, there would be room only for a 100 guests. This we expanded to 150 or so. Who all would be in this 150 posed a problem. Family guests alone numbered thirty-seven. My old physics teacher, Prof Chinnadurai, was there, as was Prof K.V. Pandalai of the Madras Institute of Technology, Pakshi Venkatasubramaniam Sastrigal, chief priest of the Rameswaram temple, Imam Nurul Khuda, of the Rameswaram mosque, Rev. A.G. Leonard, priest of the Rameswaram church, and the famous eye specialist, Dr. G. Venkataswamy, who started the Aravind Eye Institute. Also among the guests was the dancer Sonal Mansingh, as were industrialists, journalists, personal friends. In the guest list, uniquely, there were 100 children from all the states of the country, for whom there was a separate enclosure. They were put under the care of a senior aide. It was a hot day but everybody came formally dressed to attend the ceremony in the historic Central Hall.

So this was the story of a great scientist and a patriot who became the 11th President of India. Kalam, a non-politician, brought the much-needed dignity and stature to the presidency. His unprecedented popularity among the masses is seen as the biggest evidence of this fact. A people's president for sure, Kalam was also the most unconventional President Indian political history had witnessed. During his presidency, attitudes and ambience changed in the Rashtrapati Bhavan. Protocol was reduced to an executive term. The President's office staffers were always free to call upon him for discussion of issues. "If you can pick up the phone and speak, why can't you meet me in person?" this great man used to ask his officials.

Right after Dr. Abdul Kalam was elected as the President, he attended an event at Kerala Raj Bhavan in Trivandrum. With the power vested in him, he could have invited any two people as the Presidential guests. Guess who he called? A road side cobbler and the owner of a very small hotel. Dr. Kalam had spent a significant time as a scientist in Trivandrum. He invited the cobbler and the hotel owner, both of whom he was close to during his time in Kerala. No other politician can do this, can they?

Dr. Kalam was a true nature lover and his romance with Mughal Gardens is not unknown to the world. During his presidency, he had introduced some wonderful things to make the Garden a better place to visit. When in 1997, Kalam was awarded with Bharat Ratna, the highest civilian award for his contribution to the missile programme, he got a chance to visit Mughal Garden with the then president K.R. Narayanan and his daughter Chitra Narayanan. Mesmerised by the exquisite beauty of the Mughal, Kalam expressed a desire to witness its splendour under the moonlight. When Narayanan's wife came to know about the scientist's love for Mughal Garden, she made it a point that he stayed in Rashtrapati Bhawan on his succeeding visits to New Delhi for official banquet.

Kalam Sahab in his book 'Turning Points: A Journey Through Challenges' had written, "At that time, I did not realise that I was going to see more than 60 full moon nights in the Rashtrapati

Bhawan. During the time of my stay there, the Mughal Garden turned into a great place of experiment for me. It was a great communication medium between me, nature and the citizens of the country; a place where I met people from diverse walks of life, including specialists in herbal plants, for which there was a section in the estate. The birds and animals that frequented the garden became my friends and the serene and the orderly environment of the garden and its magnificent trees gave me a sense of peace."

While walking with the heads of the state of SAARC nations in the garden in the year 2007, the then Prime Minister of Pakistan Mr. Shaukat Ali had mentioned to Kalam that if the bilateral meetings are held in the Mughal Garden, the differences between the two nations will vanish into thin air.

Dr. Kalam had installed two huts in Mughal Garden. Both were constructed from natural materials. One was built by craftsmen frm Tripura and christened as 'Thinking Hut'. A significant part of book 'Indomitable Spirit' was written in this hut. The other was called the 'Immortal Hut'. One of Kalam's literary masterpieces 'Guiding Soul' emanated in the hut through regular discussions held among the president and his close friends. The place was also a source of inspiration for Kalam to pen down many of his sterling poems.

Kalam's love for nature had inspired him to add value and make new introductions to the garden. Herbal gardens were added at Kalam's initiative. The primary purpose of the herb garden developed in several phases is to create awareness about rare and endangered medicinal plants. The former president was also instrumental in creating the first tactile garden in Rashtrapati Bhavan in the year 2004 with a fountain, stone-guided path and beds of herbs, spices, fruits and aromatic flowers. It acts as a sensory garden that stimulates the senses, besides being visually appealing. Kalam used to visit this garden with the visually challenged who got thrilled to be here. Each bed has a signboard here describing the plants in Braille (Hindi and English). A musical fountain was installed here in the year 2006.

When American President George W. Bush with his wife Laura

Bush visited India, Kalam hosted a grand feast in Mughal Garden to honour the guests. The royal couple was delighted to see the arrangement.

Once Santoor Maestro played a concert in Mughal Garden under full moon night. Over 500 spectators were mesmerised to experience the amazing combination of heavenly melody and unparalleled beauty of the garden.

The humanist President Dr. A.P.J. Abdul Kalam's love towards animals is fondly remembered by all those who were close to him. He always had a soft corner to injured and handicapped animals and birds and would go to to any extent to help them. The staff of Rashtrapathi Bhavan have hundreds of instances to cite. The humanist President Dr. A.P.J. Abdul Kalam's love towards animals is fondly remembered by all those who were close to him. He always had a soft corner to injured and handicapped animals and birds and would go to to any extent to help them. The staff of Rashtrapathi Bhavan have hundreds of instances to cite.

It was Dr. Kalam's idea to open a bio-diversity park. Located adjacent to the herbal garden, the existing Deer Park was converted into the bio-diversity park. The place is home to deer, rabbits, ducks, peacocks and tortoises. The former president wanted to create a place that is peaceful. People are not allowed to just walk into this park.

Once Dr. Kalam was enjoying a casual stroll with his friend Dr. Sudhir. He saw a baby deer whose mother had abandoned it. Since two of its legs were defected by birth, it was not able to walk properly. Dr. Sudhir carried the deer to his clinic and treated it. After some time, the deer was able to walk and its clan accepted it as a part of their family. Dr. Kalam admitted that this incident touched his heart deeply. The pleasure he felt during the visit to Mughal Garden and other parks was far less than what he experienced after seeing the little deer jumping and hopping around with its new found friends.

Kalam had always dreamt of flying a fighter plane. A.P.J. Abdul

Kalam was the only Indian President to have flown supersonic on a Su-30MKI fighter aircraft for 40-minute at the Lohegaon Air Force base in Pune on June 8, 2006. The President's flight marked the airbase's 50th anniversary. The Sukhoi-30 MKI with its special payload took off as hundreds of Indian Air Force officers and some three dozen journalists watched. President Kalam co-piloted the plane with Wing Commander Ajay Rathore, commanding officer of the Lightning Squadron based at Lohegaon.

Kalam had never allowed his larger than life post to take a toll on his personality. Nevertheless as the president of India, Kalam had two paths ready for him to tread on towards the development of country and while undertaking his duties:

First to keep tabs on the activitties of functioning of government and making people in it aware of the errors and blunders committed on a regular basis.

Second to help Rashtrapati Bhawan emerge as the focal point for academic pursuits and exchange of thoughts and ideas.

For some reasons, the former president did not approach the first path. Kalam was heavily criticised for his inaction in deciding the fate of 20 out of the 21 mercy petitions submitted to him during his tenure. According to Kalam, "We are all the creation of God. I am not sure a human system of a human being is competent to take away a life based on artificial and created evidence." Thus, at the end of his five-year term, A.P.J. Abdul Kalam left behind over two dozen mercy pleas, having decided only two — rejecting the plea of rape-cum-murder convict Dhananjoy Chatterjee (2004), and commuting the death sentence of Kheraj Ram into life imprisonment (2006).

He had always said that one of the more difficult tasks for him as President was to decide on the issue of confirming capital punishment awarded by the courts after exhausting all processes of appeals.

Kalam signed a proclamation imposing president's rule on Bihar on May 23, 2005 while on a tour of Russia. This was done following a recommendation by state governor Buta Singh. The Supreme Court reversed the dissolution of the Bihar Assembly as it describe the action as unconstitutional. According to reports, Kalam was keen on overcoming his sense of remorse by putting in his papers, but ultimately decided to stay on.

Despite the simple lifestyle and unassuming disposition followed by Kalam, he loved being the President. No wonder he was quite inclined to take another shot at office. He also made his intention known, but later on stepped aside.

On a meeting with former president of Pakistan Pervez Musharraf, Kalam lectured later on some interesting subjects and even enlightened him with new subjects.

A day before meeting, Kalam's secretary briefed him about the meeting with Pervez Musharraf.

"Yes, I know," Kalam said.

"He will certainly raise the issue of Kashmir. Are you ready for it?" Nayar asked.

"Don't worry. I will handle it." Kalam paused for a moment and replied confidently.

In the year 2005, Musharraf reached Rashtrapati Bhavan for the luncheon meeting with President A P J Abdul Kalam. The Indian president welcomed his guest and exchanged pleasantries. The meeting was supposed to go on only for 30 minutes. The scientist-statesman took the general to his personal room and invited him to take a look at some of the projects he had been working on.

In a few minutes, the two presidents were busy looking at the computer holding details of his Providing Urban Amenities in the Rural Areas scheme. In the 25-minute presentation, President Kalam explained to the visiting leader how his project will bring about a change in the lives of the rural poor.

"Dear President, I believe your country too, like ours is home to several rural areas. Don't you think we must work towards their development?" Kalam asked.

Musharraf had no choice but to answer in a plain "yes". "I would like to brief you on PURA. PURA means Providing Urban facilities to Rural Areas," said Kalam and for the next 26 minutes, the two were busy staring at the presentation on plasma screen.

"Thank You, Sir," said Musharraf. "India is lucky to have a president like you."

The two shaked hands and bid adieu. Nayar noted in his diary, 'scientists can be diplomats too'.

What is PURA? The details are mentioned in Kalam's book 'India 2020'. The former president aspired to see India as one of the leading nations under the category of astronomical science. Was Kalam a politician? Well, considering the present age political scenario, he certainly was not one! A Muslim by religion, Kalam was seen playing veena and reading Bhagvad Geeta. Here, we are talking about the great personality who once struggled to collect drops of kerosene oil for survival but aimed towards making it big in the field of nuclear weapons. He always though of technical advancement and preached the need of software to be free of technical complications so that these can be used by common man of India. Kalam's presidency ended in 25 July, 2007.

His tenure as a President :
Some issues

During his term as president, he was affectionately known as the People's President.Saying that signing the Office of Profit Bill was the toughest decision he had taken during his tenure. Kalam was criticised for his inaction in deciding the fate of 20 out of the 21 mercy petitions submitted to him during his tenure. Article 72 of the Constitution of India empowers the President of India to grant pardons, and suspend or commute the death sentence of convicts on death row. Kalam acted on only one mercy plea in his five-year tenure as president, rejecting the plea of rapist Dhananjoy Chatterjee, who was later hanged. Perhaps the most notable plea was from Afzal Guru, a Kashmiri terrorist who was convicted of conspiracy in the December 2001 attack on the Indian Parliament and was sentenced to death by the Supreme Court of India in 2004. While the sentence was scheduled to be carried out on 20th October 2006, the pending action on his mercy plea resulted in him remaining on death row. He also took the controversial decision to impose President's Rule in Bihar in 2005.

Post Presidential Term

In September 2003, in an interactive session in PGI Chandigarh, Kalam supported the need of Uniform Civil Code in India, keeping in view the population of the country.

At the end of his term, on 20th June 2007, Kalam expressed his willingness to consider a second term in office provided there was certainty about his victory in the 2007 presidential election. However, two days later, he decided not to contest the Presidential election again stating that he wanted to avoid involving Rashtrapati Bhavan from any political processes. He did not have the support of the left parties, Shiv Sena and UPA constituents, to receive a renewed mandate.

Post-Presidency

The post presidency phase couldn't dampen the spirit of this great personality. He used his valuable experience and unprecedented knowledge and achieved immense fame as an educationalist, life coach, and non-political leader for the masses. The sweetness of this amzing leader's life was dedicate to awaken the spirits of Indian youth, children, and boatmen. Despite holding a prestigious post as that of president of the nation, Kalam continued to be a true educationalist and spared time to give lectures. These lectures continued post-presidency. Almost all of the seminars and lectures conducted by Kalam were attended by school going children, young men and women, journalists, politicians, and other great personalities across the nation.

I would like to quote one such lecture here. Being lucky to have been an eye witness to a lecture conducted in Bhopal in December, 2007, I can never forget the impressive words being said during the entire event. Kalam said, "Every student and educationalist must work towards acieving at least one goal in their life. This is the mantra for helping our nation emerge as a superpower."

After leaving Bijnor, Kalam served as a visiting professor at Indian Institute of Management Shillong, Indian Institute of Management Ahmedabad and Indian Institute of Management Indore, honorary fellow of Indian Institute of Science, Bangalore, Chancellor of the Indian Institute of Space Science and Technology Thiruvananthapuram, a professor of Aerospace Engineering at Anna University (Chennai), JSS University(Mysore) and an adjunct/ visiting faculty at many other academic and research institutions across India. He also taught information technology at IIIT Hyderabad and technology at Banaras Hindu University and Anna University.

In May 2012, Kalam launched a programme for the youth of

India called the What Can I Give Movement, with a central theme of defeating corruption. He also enjoyed writing Tamil poetry and playing 'Veenai', a south Indian musical instrument. In 2003 and in 2006 he was nominated for the MTV Youth Icon of the Year award.

One of the most distinguished scientists of India, Kalam has also made an indelible mark in the world of literature. In his literary pursuit Dr. Kalam authored a number of poems. This includes a beautiful collection of Tamil poems, 'Yenudaya Prayana'. had a very subtle heart of a music lover. He always cherished the rich heritage and culture of India. Music was an integral part of his life and he was an ardent fan of carnatic music. Being a fan of carnatic music, Dr. A.P.J. Abdul Kalam loved to play veena and he used to spend his spare time playing veena. The former president believed that creating library can encourage reading habit among family members which would help to create a good atmosphere in the house and give a chance among family members to have a healthy discussion on common topics, which is essential for maintaining good harmony. One of the floors of his duplex bungalow at 10 Rajaji Marg was converted into library where he had a huge collection of books related to science, music, and poems.

Kalam adored Vikram Sarabhai as his favourite scientist. Milton, Whiteman, and Rabindranath Tagore were his favourite poets. How should people remember him as – a great scientist, Tamilian, Indian, or a good human being? A good human being will be the better term. In his own words, "It comprises of all three qualities." Kalam was not just the president of naion but 'people's president'. In fact, he was the only president of India who preached the significance of humanity as the biggest religion.

Kalam remained passionate and committed to what he called Vision 2020 – transforming India with a focussed manifesto for change. His vision of a developed India was a passionate project for him which he had worked on with great enthusiasm. In April 2013, A P J Abdul Kalam launched the Madhya Pradesh government's Atal Jyoti Abhiyan aimed at providing round-the-clock quality power supply in the district. The programme was successfully implemented in six districts. Emphasising the need to conserve power for meeting future requirements, Kalam stated that traditionally, the human society has seen four levels of fuels such as wood, oil and petroleum products, nuclear energy and non-conventional energy sources including solar and wind. He said that a new concept of the fifth fuel has recently emerged, which is not a hardware fuel in the conventional sense but refers to energy efficiency. According to Kalam, several reports suggest that building energy efficiency is perhaps the most economically feasible and convenient way to generate energy by actually saving it. The former president emphasised on the fact that social awareness and incentives for the industries and homes is required more than any form of technology to save on energy consumption.

A.P.J. Abdul Kalam was passionate about the ancient Indian medicine system of Ayurveda and was keen to modernise it on a global scale. This was confirmed by the chief of an international NGO. Praful Patel, a leading light of the International Ayurveda Foundation (IAF) in India, Britain and Switzerland said that he got to know about Kalam's passion for Ayurveda after meeting him in Rashtrapati Bhavan in November, 2005.

"We discussed the many challenges facing Ayurveda in India and abroad and sought his advice. He stressed the need to set up an Ayurveda Research and Development Centre, both herbal and non-herbal products," Patel said.

Kalam desired it to be a joint effort of the Ayurvedic community and the Indian government; the centre should provide fool-proof testing and certification of Ayurvedic and other traditional medicinal products about their quality, safety, stability and efficacy.

Patel further added that Kalam was also keen to increase the production of medicinal plants of which the world produced $68 billion worth, with the Indian share barely half a billion dollars, and China standing far ahead of this country. He also recalled that Kalam stressed on India's wealth of land in southern parts....the eastern states and in Himalayas which could be encouraged for the

 Pride of the Nation: Dr. A.P.J. Abdul Kalam

mass-scale growth of medicinal plants.

The then president stated that if any large company made such an investment anywhere across the nation, they could encourage the local farming community to join their venture, purchase the medicinal plants directly from them -- something on the lines of the Amul Dairy experiment in Gujarat.

The International Ayurveda Foundation had already prepared a project report on the R&D centre and was hoping to get a syndicate which can achieve both the dream projects of Kalam. Unfortunately, before this dream project could see the light of day, the cruel cluthes of death snatched our dearest president Abdul Kalam from us.

Once again, nearing the expiry of the term of the 12th President Pratibha Patil on 24th July 2012, media reports in April claimed that Kalam was likely to be nominated for his second term. After the reports, social networking sites witnessed a number of people supporting his candidature. The BJP potentially backed his nomination, saying that the party would lend their support if the Trinamool Congress, Samajwadi Party and Indian National Congress proposed him for the 2012 presidential election. A month ahead of the election, Mulayam Singh Yadav and Mamata Banerjee also expressed their support for Kalam. Days afterwards, Mulayam Singh Yadav backed out, leaving Mamata Banerjee as the solitary supporter. On 18th June 2012, Kalam declined to contest the 2012 presidential poll. He said of his decision not to do so:

Many, many citizens have also expressed the same wish. It only reflects their love and affection for me and the aspiration of the people. I am really overwhelmed by this support. This being their wish, I respect it. I want to thank them for the trust they have in me.

After leaving office, Kalam became a visiting professor at the Indian Institute of Management Shillong, the Indian Institute of Management Ahmedabad, and the Indian Institute of Management Indore; an honorary fellow of Indian Institute of Science, Bangalore; chancellor of the Indian Institute of Space Science and Technology Thiruvananthapuram; professor of Aerospace Engineering at Anna

University; and an adjunct at many other academic and research institutions across India. He taught information technology at the International Institute of Information Technology, Hyderabad, and technology at Banaras Hindu University and Anna University.

In May 2012, Kalam launched a programme for the youth of India called the What Can I Give Movement, with a central theme of defeating corruption.

In 2011, Kalam was criticised by civil groups over his stand on the Koodankulam Nuclear Power Plant; he supported the establishment of the nuclear power plant and was accused of not speaking with the local people. The protesters were hostile to his visit as they perceived to him to be a pro-nuclear scientist and were unimpressed by the assurances provided by him regarding the safety features of the plant.

Death

President APJ Abdul Kalam, the 'missile man' who came to be known as 'People's President' died on Monday, 27th July, 2015 after he collapsed during a lecture at the IIM in Shillong on Monday evening.

Kalam, who would have turned 84 in October, was confirmed dead more than two hours after he was wheeled into the ICU of Bethany hospital in a critical condition following the collapse at around 6.30 pm. Dr. Kalam suffered a massive cardiac arrest during the lecture at IIM, Shillong.

Being considered the most popular President, Kalam became the 11th head of the state and occupied the post between 2002 and 2007 but lack of consensus denied a second term in office for a man who came from outside political spectrum.

Meghalaya Governor V. Shanmughanathan, rushed to the hospital on hearing the news of his admission.He said Kalam died at 7.45 pm. Despite medical team best efforts, he could not be revived.

Doctors from the army hospital and North Eastern Indira Gandhi Regional Institute of Health and Medical Sciences (NEIGRIHMS) rushed to Bethany hospital but their efforts proved to be of no avail.

Avul Pakir Jainulabdeen Abdul Kalam rose from humble origins to become the President in the most unexpected manner during the NDA government under Atal Bihari Vajpayee after an all party consensus minus the left parties that saw him through in an election which he won handsomely.

An aeronautics engineer from Madras Institute of Technology, Kalam was considered the brain of missile programme in India got and as Chief Scientific Adviser to Vajpayee was also instrumental in the Pokharan nuclear test in 1998.

As President, Kalam utilised any opportunity that came to him to address students, especially school children, to dream big so that they became achievers in life. A bachelor, the former President was a veena player and was deeply interested in Carnatic music. He was vegetarian all his life.

Earlier during the day, Kalam had tweeted about his function at IIM Shillong.

Going to Shillong.. to take course on Livable Planet earth at IIM. With @srijanpalsingh and Sharma.

— APJ Abdul Kalam (@APJAbdulKalam) July 27, 2015

Obituaries by leading personalities and Press

Mr Narendra Modi, Prime Minister of India

"As a scientist, Dr. Kalam has brought India to greater levels. He has been a guide in my life and I was lucky to have worked closely with him in the past."

"His death is a big loss to the world and to the world of science as well. While he was a President and even after that, Dr. Kalam maintained that he is a teacher and teaching is his passion. And even in his last few moments, he spent it with the children doing what he loved the most." He also tweeted:

India mourns the loss of a great scientist, a wonderful President & above all an inspiring individual. RIP Dr. APJ Abdul Kalam

Barack Obama- President of USA

On behalf of the American people, I wish to extend my deepest condolences to the people of India on the passing of former Indian President Dr. APJ Abdul Kalam. A scientist and statesman, Dr. Kalam rose from humble beginnings to become one of India's most accomplished leaders, earning esteem at home and abroad. An advocate for stronger U.S.-India relations, Dr. Kalam worked to deepen our space cooperation, forging links with NASA during a 1962 visit to the United States. His tenure as India's 11th president witnessed unprecedented growth in U.S.-India ties. Suitably named "the People's President," Dr. Kalam's humility and dedication to public service served as an inspiration to millions of Indians and admirers around the world.

Mark Tully- The Guardian

The president of India is constitutional head of state, an office in many ways similar to the British crown. Like British monarchs, Indian presidents are housed in a vast palace and usually surrounded by stifling ceremonial. APJ Abdul Kalam was an extraordinary president of India, in office from 2002 until 2007. He became known as the "people's president" because he welcomed the public into the palace in New Delhi (built for the last of the viceroys by the British architect Sir Edwin Lutyens) and made himself accessible whenever he travelled. Kalam, who has died aged 83, was unusual, too, in that he never held any political ambitions.

He was also an extraordinary scientist, known as the "missile man", who played a crucial role in India's most successful programmes. In the words of one of his former colleagues: "The success of our space programme, our missile development and our nuclear weaponry all owe their genesis to him." Yet he had studied aeronautical engineering at the Madras Institute of Technology when it was a technology college, not a university, and never took a postgraduate degree.

Son of Jainulabdeen and Ashiamma, Kalam was born in the small temple town of Rameswaram on the southern coast. His father, who owned a boat, had no academic qualifications but was deeply interested in religion; a Muslim himself, he used to hold regular meetings in his house with a Christian and a Hindu priest. Kalam said it was from their discussions that he learned what he called "true secularism".

He went to a Catholic school, St Joseph's college, in another southern temple town, Tiruchirappalli, formerly Trichinopoly. He studied physics there, but was not an outstanding student. After leaving the Madras Institute of Technology in 1960, he joined the Defence Research and Development Organisation, and his subsequent scientific career was spent in government research organisations. In most of these, scientists are hampered by bureaucratic procedures and political interference. Kalam developed the skill of protecting his scientists without falling out of favour.

He held a series of prestigious posts, including project director for India's first indigenous satellite launch vehicle, and chief of the integrated guided missile development programme. From 1992 until 1999 he was chief scientific adviser to the prime minister and the defence minister. In 1998 he was the chief project co-ordinator for India's second nuclear test. The year before that he was awarded the Bharat Ratna, India's highest civilian honour.

In 2002 there was a disagreement between the two biggest political parties, the rightwing Hindu Bharatiya Janata party, or BJP, which was in power, and the Nehru-Gandhi family's Congress party, over the choice of politician to be elected president. The then BJP prime minister, Atal Bihari Vajpayee, broke the logjam by offering the presidency to Kalam. The Congress realised they could not object to him.

Kalam took his duties as president extremely seriously. Under the Indian constitution, all bills have to be approved by the president before they become acts. Kalam scrutinised all those sent to him carefully and in 2006 rejected one allowing parliamentarians to hold paid public positions.

A controversy had arisen engulfing, among others, the Congress party president and MP Sonia Gandhi, widow of the former prime minister Rajiv Gandhi. The bill had been hastily prepared to find a way out of the difficulty and a committee Kalam had set up to advise him maintained that it was unconstitutional. But when the bill was returned to him, he signed, because he did not have the power to reject it twice. Later he said that signing the bill had been the hardest decision of his presidency.

The presidency did not change him. He kept his long hair, which curled round on his forehead – a close friend of his told me he had it cut only twice a year. He found time for his own pursuits, including playing the rudra-veena, an Indian classical instrument.

After his retirement Kalam remained a public figure, accepting invitations from all over India to speak, particularly to students and children. Throughout his time in office he had sought to make the presidency relevant to young people, and afterwards spoke of himself as a teacher.

Kalam is survived by a brother.

The Telegraph

APJ Abdul Kalam, who has died aged 83, was a former paper boy who became a national hero in India as the architect of the country's nuclear missile programme; in 2002 he was overwhelmingly elected India's 12th president, becoming the third Muslim to hold the post.

Kalam rose to fame in May 1998, when he oversaw five nuclear tests in the Pokhran desert which proved beyond doubt that India was capable of obliterating its old enemy Pakistan, should it feel the need. Sanctions against India were imposed by several countries, including Japan and the United States. Most Indians, however, greeted the tests with patriotic rejoicing, and Kalam became known by his tabloid sobriquet "Missile Man".

Kalam never had any regrets about his role, claiming India's nuclear programme had helped to prevent war with Pakistan: "In our planet only weaponised states are friends. Strength respects strength."

A vegetarian bachelor with thick, grey shoulder-length hair, a wardrobe which favoured short-sleeve shirts and flip-flop sandals, and a heavy Tamil accent, Kalam was an unlikely candidate for India's largely ceremonial presidency.

His election by nearly 90 per cent of the national and state legislatures completed an astonishing journey for the son of a poor boatman from south India whose sister was said to have pawned her wedding jewellery to pay for his education. Even more extraordinarily he was nominated for the post by India's ruling Hindu nationalist Bharatiya Janata Party (BJP).

APJ Abdul Kalam in 2014 (REX)

Avul Pakir Jainulabdeen Abdul Kalam was born on October 15 1931 in the small coastal temple town of Rameshwaram, now in the southern Indian state of Tamil Nadu. Abdul's ancestors had converted to Islam after contact with Arab traders who settled along India's coastal areas hundreds of years earlier.

Although he remained a Muslim, he was moulded in the tolerant traditions of Sufism and his attitudes and tastes reflected the more heterogeneous culture of India. Indeed, he enjoyed a special status in the Hindu Rameshwaram temple because one of his ancestors had dived in and retrieved its main idol from a water tank.

When he was a child, a Brahmin Hindu neighbour became Kalam's mentor and as a result of the man's influence, he became a vegetarian and teetotaller. Not only could he read Sanskrit, he could recite from the Bhagavad Gita, as well as the Koran. When he became a candidate for the Indian presidency, he even won the support of the BJP's powerful Hindu revivalist wing, one member describing him as "a Muslim with a Hindu soul".

Kalam's interest in military technology was fired by an article he read as a school boy about the Supermarine Spitfire, Britain's Second World War fighter.

His first job was as a paper boy, but he then trained as an aeronautical engineer at the Madras Institute of Technology, before joining India's fledgling space programme, where he became involved in designing satellites.

In the 1980s and 1990s he headed India's missile programme, developing its indigenous nuclear-capable Agni and Prithvi missiles. He also helped develop a low-cost coronary stent and co-designed a rough and ready tablet computer for health care workers in rural areas. He went on to become principal scientific officer to India's BJP prime Minister Atal Bihari Vajpayee.

As president Kalam made it a priority to meet, one-to-one, as many young people as possible, setting a target of 500,000 for his five-year term. Even after leaving office in 2007, "Kalam Chacha" ("Uncle Kalam"), as he became known, would receive hundreds of emails a day from young people inspired by his exhortation to "dream, dream, dream!". It is said that he replied in person to nearly all of them.

APJ Abdul Kalam, born October 15 1931, died July 27 2015

Pakistan

Pakistan today condoled the death of former president APJ Abdul Kalam, saying he would be remembered for his meritorious services.

"The Government of Pakistan expresses its condolences on the demise of Dr. A P J Abdul Kalam, former President of the Republic of India," the Foreign Office said.

"Dr. Kalam will be remembered for his meritorious services for his country," it said in a statement.

Dr. Kalam, 83, also known as India's 'missile man', collapsed during a lecture at the Indian Institute of Management in Shillong this evening and later died in a hospital.

Dr. Kalam served as the President of India from 2002 to 2007.

Obituaries from common people

One month has passed since last words you made...

No colours of the memory rainbow will fade...

no moments from the soft sand of time shall fuse...

no lessons from mosaic of wisdom has come loose.

Tides of clockwork, whispers of worldly affair...

Today, my mind goes back four weeks when Dr. Kalam and I had worked together for a message from him for today (15th August). This was to be given to a publisher and had also asked me to share it on www.givinglight.in and other online platforms on the independence day. here it is.

"As India is poised to celebrate its 69th independence day, it stands at an important moment in its history. Today India as a nation, is the 3rd largest economy, considered amongst the most promising 'emerging nations'.

Last year, we reached Mars in the most economical space program, six years after we reached the moon where we found water. This gave us a place amongst the top nations in technology.

68 years ago, when India got independence there would have been few takers abroad that one day this new democracy would achieve so much with so little investment. Independence Day is a time to reflect and appreciate the dreams, efforts and success of the visionaries of the nation and the people who toiled hard to bring us where we stand today.

Going forward our challenge remains to solve the problem of the Base of Pyramid and impoverished, of educating the quarter of our population left away from the light of knowledge and of ensuring a secured future to our farmers. It is imperative to skill our youth with global skills and make them creative in their thoughts and righteous in the heart.

Now, we are half a decade away from vision of achieving an economically developed India by 2020 – and hence all forces of democracy must gear towards this milestone through an integrated action for the nation.

–Kalam"

From Srijanpal Singh- his young advisor after his death

I write this obituary from the C-130 Air force plane with Dr. Kalam's mortal remains a few feet behind me to be taken to Rameshwaram. He is draped in the national flag, the tricolor he served and deserves. He was the hero of my generation – I remember how I used to be glued to his Presidential address just as I was finishing school. He was an ocean of experience, ideas and motivation and to capture his personality and contributions in a few hundred words is a near impossible task. But as Dr. Kalam always said, "don't stop trying" so here goes my attempt.

–Srijan Pal Singh

Most touching tribute

"Funny guy! Are you smashing?" This is what I would hear from Dr. Kalam at every single dinner or lunch we had together. "Smashing" was the typical "Kalam call-sign" for asking whether the food was good. "Funny guy" was of course a more complicated expression, which could mean a whole variety of things. Depending on the tone in which it was said, it could mean good, not good, embarrassing or simply a casual reference. If you were working with Dr. Kalam, being able to decipher his usage of the word "funny" was almost a mandatory art to know which could be learnt only through experience. It took me a good one year to figure it out! Funny!

Dr. Kalam was a teacher, mentor, guide, co-author, friend, boss from whom I received care like a mother and concern like a father. I had the great fortune of working with him closely, travelling with him so frequently for over six years, till the point he left us all. He was infectiously optimistic, to him there was never an end. He never really watched TV, but still was a cricket fan – asking me scores on matches when we travelled between functions. His favorite cricketers were Dhoni and Sachin. I remember if I told him India was not doing well in a particular match, he would reply, "Watch! Our captain will come and do something unique."

Uniqueness was so common to him. He had a voracious appetite for knowledge. The library and reading room occupying half of his 10 Rajaji Road House would be spilling books into bedroom and sometimes right upto the garden. He never departed on a journey without carrying a couple of books in his hand baggage. On the very last day of life, I remember lifting his hand baggage – it was heavy. I said, "Sir! Your bag is getting heavier!" He replied, "That is because I am reading more!"

To me the line which separated Dr. Kalam from the rest was not just his knowledge. It was his sensitivity and humility. He always introduced everybody as friend — whether it be his secretaries, his driver, his gardener, his cook or the people who maintained his house or even a stranger he just met. To him the world was truly flat, and there was no place for hierarchies and ranks in his life. I have had lunch and dinner with him at least 2000 times – often being the second to come to the table. Not once did he start eating on his own, not once did he miss asking whether I was liking the food.

　　　　　　　Pride of the Nation: Dr. A.P.J. Abdul Kalam

He had the gift of empathy – and his memory of other people's difficulties was impeccable. That was his art of winning over people. If he saw anyone with even with a small cold on a day he would offer you medicine or hot soup. The next day his first words would be – "Are you repaired?" No matter what you replied, his reaction would be, "Funny fellow you are!"

Dr. Kalam's greatest faith was the nation and its youth. Even in the final two hours of his life, we discussed on terrorism as a threat to sustainability and the issue of Parliament becoming dysfunctional – two recent pieces of news which had pained him the most. He trusted the youth, particularly his students, to come up with a solution for these issues. He was an eternal believer in the power of the ignited mind of the youth – which he termed as most powerful, on the earth, above the earth and under the earth.

What next? We are bereft of Dr. Kalam as a physical form but we are still blessed with Dr. Kalam as an idea, a vision and a dream. His thoughts and missions about empowering rural areas, about clean energy, about value based education, about creativity, innovation and integrity are still flying high.

When I was his student in 2008 at IIMA, he told me in an after-class conversation, "If you are blessed with intelligence, and empowered with education – it is your responsibility to change the world". That statement changed my life. He often said, "My dream is to see a billion smiles on billion faces". Let us give our eternally optimistic, grand old friend, inspiration, mentor and beloved People's President of the nation a reason to smile, wherever he is now. Salute you Kalam sir!

Srijan Pal Singh was an advisor to Dr. A.P.J. Abdul Kalam.

Combination of Science
and Spiritualism

Dr. Kalam believed that the fire weapons of today are only the modified forms of the 'Agni Ban' used in the ancient Vedic Age. He says that the missiles have not been discovered in the western countries, but they are the inventions of the ancient India. The names of some weapons (Astra) that we read today in the holy books like the Ramayana and the Mahabharata, —the 'Brahmastra', 'Agneyastra', Varunastra etc. — were only the missiles of the ancient India. The sole difference is that they were operated with the help of 'mantras' then and these days they are operated through modified machines.

When talked about the science of universe, Dr. Kalam said that the planets of the solar system have great effect on the human life. There are some who mislead people under the cover of astrology in a wrong way. He said, "I am not opposed to astrology as an art, but I would never support if it is taken wrongly under science, I don't know how these falsehoods about the plants, stars, constellations, and even satellites have come in existence."

Dr. Kalam said that the earth is the strongest planet which is full of energy. Every individual has a unique natural frequency to generate pulsation. It is insignificantly within you. Only you can identify it. There is no doubt in it that if religion stays on beliefs and spiritualism, science stays on materialism. The former believes in an invisible power and the latter in visible powers. Spiritualism is that science which believes in invisible. Even though science and religion are two different things, we can understand them with the help of the two.

Spiritualism means to study oneself. It can also be taken as study of spirits (soul). A spirit neither dies nor can it be killed because it is eternal, unborn, immortal and antique. It is not destroyed even if the body is. It occupies a new body leaving the old one. Neither can it be pierced by weapons, burnt by fire, drowned by water nor dried by air.

On the other hand science has proved that energy can neither be created nor destroyed. It can only be transformed from one form to the other. We find in the form of light, sound, heat, electricity and mechanics. All these forms of energy are interchangeable.

The sun is the prime source of energy which provides us the energy in the form of heat and light. The sun is adorable to science and also to religion. 'Suryashtak' and Aditya Hridaya Stotra' have been composed to worship the sun in which the greatness of the sun is praised.

Astronomy and astrology are centred around the sun. Day and night are based on the sun. Green plants receive energy from the sun and give us flowers, fruits, vegetables and cereals performing photosynthesis. Thus both science and religion believe that the creation is due to the sun. In this way we find that both energy and spirit are similar as they can neither be created nor destroyed.

According to Dr. Kalam spirit is also a form of energy. After the spirit (soul) moves out the body becomes lifeless, powerless, lustreless and energy- less. The immortality, antiquity and eternity of both energy and spirit can be taken as an extraordinary similarity between religion and science.

Today, solar energy is used in many ways. Dr. Kalam was curious to know about the science of the universe even today. He believes that there is life and movement on the planets. The physicists have proved that there is inter-atomic motion in inorganics like rocks, metals, wood or clay. Science says that electrons are constantly moving around every nucleus. The nucleus forces the electrons to remain around it. This force brings them closer. The stronger the force, the faster is the movement of electron in the orbit. In fact this movement can grow into a speed of even 1000 km/sec. This high speed makes the atom look like a solid sphere in the same way as a fast moving fan appears to be a round plate.

Dr. Kalam said that every solid has a lot of inter-molecular gaps and there is continuous movement within every still object in the same way as there is non-stop vibration of respiration at every moment of our life.

It is quite doubtful that anybody other than Dr. Kalam would have done so beautiful and fine effective analysis of the comparative combination of religion and science. Scientists have always taken these two as two different aspects, but it is Dr. Kalam only who has tried to look at their combination.

Dr. Kalam has called religion as the complement of science and vice-versa. This illuminates his minute thinking, farsightedness, his studying and analysing the ancient books, his belief and inherited culture that have positioned him at the optimum—President Kalam from a simple Kalam.

An Inspiration to future generations

India's 'missile-man' Dr. A.P.J. Abdul Kalam mentioned 'Dream India' during all his statements and explanations every now and then. He found his dreams of childhood come true. Now he wants to see his India as a leading developed nation of the world by 2020. India can fulfil his dream following his footsteps. The portrait of his 'Dream-India' is visible in his statements during his Hyderabad visit. Every Indian must read his this statement (speech):

"During our 3000 years long history different invaders from different corners of the world attacked our country. They captured our land and ruled over our brains. Right from Alexander, the Greek, the Turk, the Mughal, the Portuguese, the French, the British and the Dutch came here. They plundered and forcibly captured our motherland. But we never did this with any of the countries of the world. We never tried to impose our supremacy on others. We neither did rob them of their land, history, civilization or culture nor did we try to influence their life routine.

"Why? It is so because we know how to honour others' freedom. This is why my first vision for India is 'Freedom'. I think India got the first glimpse of freedom in 1857 when we started our freedom struggle. This is that freedom which we have to nourish, protect and maintain (nurture). If we are not independent none will respect (honour) us.

"My second vision for India is Development. We have become a developing nation in fifty years. Now it is time we should include our country in the category of developed nations of the world.

- We are among the top five countries of the world on the basis of GDP.

- Our rate of development is 10% in most of the areas.

- Our poverty level is continuously falling down.

- Our achievements are being praised thoughout the world.

"Still we lack in confidence. Are the above conditions not sufficient for looking into the direction of making India confident, self-sufficient and a developed nation?

"My third vision is to present India as a powerful nation before the world. It is so because I know none other will give us proper respect unless we are strong. Might honours might only. We have to become strong, not only as a military power but also as an economic power. Both the powers must go hand-in-hand.

"It was my good luck that I got an opportunity to work with three great personalities—Dr. Vikram Sarabhai, his heir Prof. Satish Dhawan and the originator of nuclear matters, Dr. Brahma Prakash. Luckily I got the great opportunity to work very closely with them and thereby improve my life.

"I visualise four milestones of my life:

One—I spent 20 long years in ISRO. I got the chance of becoming the Project Director of India's first Satellite Launch Vehicle, SLV-3. The 'Rohini' satellite was established in the orbit in this duration only. These years played a vital role in my life as a scientist. This was the first benediction on me.

Two—I got attached with DRDO after ISRO where I got the chance of becoming a part of India's missile programmes. The 'Agni' campaign was the second blessing on me.

Three—The Atomic Energy Department and the DRDO co-operated with each other very closely during the nuclear test-fires on 11th and 13th May 1998. This was the third blessing on me. It was a great delight for me to be a part of the team that executed these nuclear testfires. At the same time it was a matter of pride to show the world that India was not merely a developing nation but had become one among them as she was able to make such nuclear weapons. I was filled with pride of being an Indian after this incidence. In fact we have developed a very light matter, carbon-carbon to be used in 'Agni.

Four—One day an orthopedic surgeon related to disability treatment came to my laboratory from the Nizam Institute of Medical Science. He picked up that material and noted that it was very light in weight. He took me to his hospital and showed his patients. There he pointed to the young children. Boys and girls of young age were trailing having metallic callipers weighing 3 kg each tied to their feet. He requested, "Please relieve them from their agony."

We made Floor Reaction Orthosis Callipers weighing only 300 grams each within three weeks and took them to the Orthopaedic Centre. The young children could not believe their eyes (the weight of the callipers had reduced from 3 kg. to only 300 grams). In spite of dragging the weight of 3 kg. with their feet they were freely moving here and there with great ease. Their parents were touched to the hearts and tears rolled down from their eyes. This was the fourth blessing on me.

* Why our media is so inactive?

* Why do we hesitate to identify our potential and achievements and in having confidence on them?

* Our country is a great nation. Many wonderful achievements of success are in our credit. Why do we deny them?

* We are the second largest producer of wheat.

* We are also the second largest producer of rice.

* We are the first in milk production.

* We are the first in the production of remote sensing satellites.

"See Dr. Sudarshan who has made the tribal villages self- fed and self-sufficient units. Lakhs of such achievements are associated to us, but our media is obsessed with shoddy news, failures and destructions. I was reading a newspaper during my stay in Tel Aviv. There had been many attacks, bombings and deaths there only the previous day. But on the first page of the newspaper there was the photo of a Jew who had converted his desert land into a very fertile green land in a span of only five years. This was such an inspiring photograph which could inspire everyone. News of violence and other mischiefs on the inner pages covered under other news.

"In India we only read about deaths, sicknesses, poverty, terrorism and crime. Why are we so negative?

"One more question: Why are we so obsessed towards foreign goods? Why do we wish to have foreign T.V., foreign shirts etc.? We ask for foreign techniques. Why is there such obsession about imported goods? Why don't we understand that self-respect originates from self-confidence?

"A 14-year-old girl asked for my autograph when I was giving this speech in Hyderabad. I asked her what was the ambition of her life. She replied, "I want to live in developed India."

"You and I can jointly make developed India for her. You have to prove it.

"You have to accept this truth: India is not an underdeveloped nation; it is a highly developed nation."

Kalam's Call: Come,
Let's elevate the nation!

Ex-President Dr. Abdul Kalam was determined to elevate India and to make it a developed country. His address on the occasion of the last Republic Day exposed many a fact. The future India which is in our vision now will become a super power of economy, trade, technology and development because these are the dominating factors of the modern world. Therefore, the President Dr. Kalam's message to the nation on the eve of the Republic Day expressed the Vision of future India in spite of exposing the present challenges. We are well acquainted with his dream of making India a developed nation by 2020. If, like Dr. Kalam the political parties also can understand the expectations of more than half the population, people below 25 years of age, it will be the beginning of the new awareness. As Dr. Kalam told that this young generation wanted to live in a developed India and dreams of a corruption-free nation, the political parties must keep these things in the centre of their proceedings and should present the agenda of development accordingly. It is clear that Dr. Kalam invokes a change in the political thoughts without which development of India is not possible. Therefore he was asking all the parties to put up the challenge of producing alternative agenda of development before the government in spite of criticising the Government. Will the political parties heed of his call? Of course, they will, only if the voters understand their own potential and elect only those who are interested in national development. None of the fields related to the nation's welfare is untouched by the President's anxieties, be it the mishaps in the CAT examination or be it the influence on the Indian brand of higher education.

We will be able to make such a mirror from the introduction of the need and expectations of a modernised, developed and talented India to which the world will look at and praise us. India, which is unparalleled in its knowledge that does not want to look behind, that recites the hymns of peace and development, whose source of strength is a billion of its energetic people going to become the leader of the developed world.

Dr. Kalam often said in his speeches, "The youth of the country wish to live in a developed and corruption-free-India. I can notice this shining in their eyes. We can make a number of laws in the country, but none of them can uproot corruption from the country. There are only three members of the society who can do it. They are mother, father and primary teacher." He has named this plan of corruption eradication as the three-dimensional plan.

Dr. Kalam said that peace is the biggest need for development of the nation and to raise the economy of the sub-continent. He explains it through the following poem:

'When Guns are quiet,

Flowers blosson on the earth

Odorous are the holy spirits

who have created this quiet.'

Dr. Kalam, mentioning the fast growing economy of country, said, "The rural areas should also get the profit of the developing economy now. The interest rates of the banks should be determined according to smaller industries and agriculture and food preservation industry. He puts stress on the need of generating electricity by non-conventional ways apart from tripling the present electricity generation of 1 lakh megawatt units by 2020. Talking on the need of another green revolution he says it can occur by making the agriculture technology according to the farmers and encouraging their contribution in food preservation and marketing. He urges immediate action on providing education to children through electronic knowledge and remote education, appointment of better teachers and making the basic facilities available in schools. He

	Pride of the Nation: Dr. A.P.J. Abdul Kalam

supports the Indian space programmes to reach Mars and not limit it upto the moon only.

Let Us Make Such a Nation Jointly

- Which is the best study centre for brilliant students and scientists.

- Which is the best place to live in on the earth and where there is smile on the faces of the one billion people.

- Where agriculture, industry and service sectors use such technologies that the maximum wealth can be earned and job opportunities can be increased.

- Which is healthy, prosperous, secured, peaceful and well-off.

- Where everybody gets water and electricity equally.

- Where all get good and immediate health facilities and AIDS, T.B., cancer, heart diseases and water-borne diseases are uprooted.

- Where the difference between a city and a village diminishes.

- Where there is no poverty, illiteracy and atrocity on women and all live in peace and harmony in the society.

- Where talented students should not have to face the problem of social and economic indiscrimination in obtaining education.

- Where government uses the best technology and is fully transparent, easily accessible and corruption-free.

- Oath by the Youth of the Country

- I will never support any indiscrimination based on religion, caste or language.

- I shall plant at least ten trees and take good and regular care of them.

- I shall treat the mentally retarded and physically disabled persons like a friend and help them lead normal life.

- I shall take up my education and work with firm adherence and shall try to become the best.

- I shall always try to relieve sick people.

- I shall teach at least ten illiterates to read and write.

- I shall feel proud on the success of our country and countrymen.

- I shall work to become a conscious citizen and make my family an ideal one.

- I shall work for the acquittal of at least ten people from their bad habits of toxication and gambling in the villages and the cities.

- I shall become honest and try to make a corruption-free society.

Web-site of the Rashtrapati Bhawan

President Dr. A.P.J. Abdul Kalam restarted the Website of the Indian President. Some new features were added to it. There was a special arrangement for children so that they can ask questions to the President without accessing to the E-mail. At the same time any of the Indian citizens could straightaway ask questions to the President through the web-site. This web-site had separate class of Press communiques where they are mentioned with dates. There was a media gallery in which current pictures were shown. Zip, power point slides and PDF files showed the speeches and statements. The web-site included information about the President of India, the Rashtrapati Bhawan, former Presidents, messages to the nation, Parliamnetary addresses, special speeches, etc. The new version of this web-site is presidentofindia.nic.in

Two Inspiring Poems by Dr. Kalam

Song of Youth

As a young citizen of India, armed with technology, knowledge and love for my nation, I realize, small aim is a crime.

I will work and sweat for a great vision, the vision of transforming India into a developed nation, powered by economic strength with value system.

I am one of the citizens of the billion; Only the vision will ignite the billion souls,

It has entered into me; The ignited soul compared to any resource is the most powerful resource on the earth, above the earth and under the earth.

I will keep the lamp of knowledge burning to achieve the vision - Developed India.

If we work and sweat for the great vision with ignited minds, the transformation leading to the birth of vibrant developed India will happen.

I pray the Almighty: "May the divine peace with beauty enter into our people;

Happiness and good health blossom in our bodies, minds and souls".

My National Prayer

The grand Scene of birth of Independent India In that midnight, the flag of the ruler of two centuries lowered; The tri-color Indian flag flaps in the Red Fort in the midst of National Anthem.

The first vision of Independent India was dawned.

The rejoice everywhere, happiness all around, there was a tender cry: where is the father of the nation? The white clothed soul walking in the midst of sorrows and pain, Injected by hatred and ego, the result of communal violence.

The father of the nation, Mahatma, walking bare footed In the streets of Bengal for peace and harmony, With the strength of blessed soul of Mahatma I pray the Almighty: When will be the dawn of second vision?

Create thoughts in the minds of my people, and transform those thoughts into action. Embed the thought of Nation being bigger than the individual, in the minds of leaders and people.

Help all the leaders of my country to give strength And bless the nation with peace and prosperity. Give strength to all my religious leaders to bring 'Unity of Minds' among all our billion people.

Oh! Almighty, bless all my people to work and transform our country from a developing into a developed nation. Let this second vision be born out of sweat of my people, and bless our youth to live in Developed India.

Dr. Kalam's Speeches — I

(At N.F.S.S. Valedictory Function)

I am delighted to participate in the vale-dictory function of the National Food Security Summit which is aiming to achieve the national goal of hunger-free India by 15th August 2007. I greet the scientists, technologists, policy makers, distinguished guests and all those including our farming community who are associated with this noble task of providing food security to the billion people.

I am very happy to attend the Food Security Summit organized by M.S. Swaminathan Research Foundation. Our country had demonstrated that food security is the foundation of our economic security and economic security leads to national security and other forms of social security like health security and education and employment opportunity. I would like to narrate two incidents which happened a few years back. In one case, I was involved directly in the development of technology, in the other I was in the government policy making and management. One was with operationalization of Agni, the long range missile and the second was the five consecutive nuclear tests which took place in Pokhran on May 11, 1998. The combination of these two events led India to declare itself as a nuclear weapon state. Within three days of our declaration, all the developed countries, except one or two, clamped on India both technological and economical sanctions. This led to the suspension of contracts and agreements in which both the countries were working together, such as the ICA contract.

The World Bank economic loans were kept in abeyance. The industries were denied components and devices including computer systems, software's, its patches and its upgrades. Number of Indian companies, which were declared as entities, could not import even ordinary maintenance items for the equipments which had been imported before. For example, the five-axis CNC Machine was denied even for civil applications. In this situation, I would like to share with our youth how India came out of the chaos created by the developed world. The three strengths, namely technological strength, leadership strength and concerted effort made by the Indians got us out of trouble. How this was possible? Let us see the major elements.

Firstly, we had sufficient food stocks in our country and our production capacity was excellent. Secondly, our information and communication technology area had shown excellent performance even in a denied market. Thirdly, our NRIs came to our rescue by oversubscribing to the resurgent India Bond (RIB) scheme launched by State Bank of India. Above all the leadership in India, both ruling parties and opposition parties, defended India's external policies and stood as a rock for the country's national interests. Therefore, we came out successful. Today, not only the nation has become stronger in national security areas, due to our standing firm on our principles and ideals of our nation, we have also become economically stronger. This incident demonstrates our spirit of "We can do it" resulting in the ascent phase of our economic prosperity being experienced today. I have chosen my theme as "PURA In Action".

Vision 2020: Developed India as a Mission

As you are aware we have in our nation 260 million people living below the poverty line. The nation has to lift them up. Today the GDP growth rate is about 6%; it has to be lifted up to 10% and to be sustained for several years. Then it is possible for India to get developed economically and the billion people will feel the prosperity of the nation. The roadmap involves integrated action on the following five areas:

(1) Agriculture and food processing—We have to place a target of 360 million tonnes of food and agricultural production. Other

    Pride of the Nation: Dr. A.P.J. Abdul Kalam

areas of agriculture and agro food processing would bring prosperity to rural people and speed up economic growth. (2) Reliable and quality electric power for all parts of the country. (3) Education and healthcare— We have seen, based on experience, education and healthcare are inter-related. (4) Information and communication technology - This is one of our core competencies. We believe this area can be used to promote education in remote areas and also to create national wealth. (5) Strategic sectors—

This area, fortunately, witnessed growth in nuclear technology, space technology and defence technology.

These areas have been converted into missions such as: Networking of rivers, availability of high quality uninterrupted power, Providing Urban Amenities in Rural Areas (PURA).

Second Green Revolution, Information and Communication Technology (ICT) transforming into knowledge products and tourism. These specific integrated missions sector-wise will take the country forward on the path to self- sustaining development. These missions will provide the thrust for the realization of developed India in a time-bound manner. They will also provide large-scale employment opportunities for the youth through creation of various types of industries and enhancement of the national infrastructure. Many young persons with professional education can become entrepreneurs themselves, thus contributing to economic growth and creation of new avenues of employment.

Food Security

Food security can be studied from three different view points. First, availability of food, which depends upon production and distribution; second, access to food that is guided by purchasing power; and third, food absorption. Food absorption implies being able to assimilate the food consumed in order to live a healthy and long life. This can come about with good sanitation facilities and better health care infrastructure. For enhanced production and distribution, we have to immediately launch the second green revolution.

Agriculture and Agro Food Processing

India has to now embark upon the Second Green Revolution which will enable it to further increase its productivity and diversity in the agricultural sector. The second green revolution will have the fanners in focus, fanning technology as the friend, food processing and marketing as partners and the consumers as the angels to be satisfied. From now on to 2020, India would have to gradually increase the production to around 400 million tonnes of grains. The increase in the production will have to be done under the reduced availability of land from 170 million hectares to 100 million hectares with reduced water availability. We should also learn to diversify to meet specific consumer preferences, export markets and also in the interest of ecological balance. This is be achieved through information access to all stakeholders and not with central controls or restriction of movements of agro products.

The challenges for the scientists and technologies would be in the areas of development of seeds that would ensure good yield even under constraints of water and land with ecologically balanced farming. The challenges for the scientists is indeed a knowledge graduation from characterization of soil to the matching of the seed with the composition of the fertilizer, water management and evolving new pre-harvesting techniques for such conditions. The domain of farming would enlarge from grain production to food processing and marketing. Newer forms of co-operative entities are required to be established for ensuring maximum benefit to the farmers. E-marketing concepts may also be put into practice to provide farmers choices in selling. Some of the areas which need focus are: soil upgradation, dry land agriculture, temperature and salinity resistant seeds and minimum water cultivation. There have been successful experiments carried out by TIFAC team in Bihar, where per hectare output of wheat has been tripled by farmers in collaboration with agriculture scientists through scientific methods. Such experiments can be replicated in many parts of our country, carefully tailored to local conditions. The earning of the participating farmers have remarkably improved. This is a crucial socio-economic need. Access to food will need enhancement of purchasing power of the rural and urban population. This can only come out of employment generation through entrepreneurship and through increase in the incomes of existing farmers by techniques adopted by the TIFAC team briefly mentioned above.

Employment Generation through Entrepreneurship

There has been substantial growth in our higher educational system and we are generating over 3 million graduates every year. However our employment generation system is not in a position to absorb the graduates passing out from the universities leading to increase in educated unemployed, year after year. There is a large mismatch between the skills required for the modern economy and the education imparted to most of these students. This situation will lead to instability in the social structure. We need higher education focused on and oriented towards employment opportunities. A multi-pronged strategy is needed to make education more attractive and simultaneously create employment potential. How do we do that?

Firstly, the educational system should highlight the importance of entrepreneurship and prepare the students right from the college education to get oriented towards setting up of the enterprises which will provide them creativity, freedom and ability to generate wealth. Diversity of skills and perseverance in work makes an entrepreneur. It should be taught to all the students. In addition, college syllabi even for arts, science, and commerce courses should include topics and practicals where such entrepreneurship is possible. Secondly, the banking system should provide venture capital right from every village level to the prospective entrepreneurs for undertaking new enterprises. Banks have to be proactive to support the innovative products for enabling wealth generation by young entrepreneurs by setting aside the "conventional tangible asset syndrome". Definitely this involves certain amount of calculated risks which can be eliminated by making an analysis of successful venture capital enterprises. Thirdly, there has to be an economic pull for human resources; for example, generation of marketable products and enhancement of purchasing power among the people. This can come through the implementation of mega programmes such as PURA, Interlinking of Rivers, Infrastructural Mission, Power Mission and Tourism. Also genuine and competitive border trade can increase if we have a friendly border in all sectors.

The educational institutions, Government and the private enterprises should become facilitators for creating this entrepreneurship scheme through the support of the banking system and the marketing system. This is one way of reducing the employment gap leading to upliftment of the 260 million people living below the poverty line.

PURA Concept

The cabinet in its meeting on 20th January 2004 has accorded in principle approval for execution of PURA (Providing Urban Amenities in Rural Areas) within the existing gross budgetary support for bridging the rural-urban divide and achieving balanced socio-economic development. This scheme is proposed to be implemented in 4130 rural clusters across the country in the next five years. The north- eastern states, other special category states and backward areas, identified by the Planning Commission, would get priority under the scheme.

Economic Connectivity for PURA

Providing Urban facilities in Rural Areas (PURA) consisting of four connectivities; physical, electronic, knowledge and thereby leading to economic connectivity to enhance the prosperity of clusters of villages in the rural areas. The economic connectivity will generate a market and the production establishments for servicing the market. The PURA has all the dimensions to become a business enterprise, which has global dimensions but operating in every nook and corner of our country. The PURA entrepreneur has to have the skill for evolving a business plan with banks and also create infrastructural support such as educational institutions, health centres and small scale industries, transportation services, tele-education, tele-medicine, e-governance services in the region integrating with the government rural development schemes such as road, communication and transport and also with national and global markets to sell the products and services.

PURA Model

Depending upon the region and the state of present development PURA can be classified in three different categories, namely Type A, Type B, Type C—PURA Clusters. The characteristic features of these types are given below:

For example, Type A Cluster is situated closer to an urban area and having minimal road connectivity, limited infrastructure, limited support—school, primary health centre. Type B Cluster is situated closer to urban area but has sparsely spread infrastructure and no connectivity, Type C Cluster is located far interior with no infrastructure, no connectivity and no basic amenities.

Criteria for PURA Clusters

Type A Cluster may be with the Population of 30,000 to 1,00,000 in about 10 to 15 villages with adequate land for 4- lane circular road, without having canals, rail and power line obstacles, ensuring minimum displacement of people, and preferably falls within the district jurisdiction. Similar criteria need to be worked out for B and C Clusters. A typical PURA. Cluster may have the following specifications:

PURA Enterprise

The small and medium industry enterprises in India have experience in managing the small and medium scale industries of different types in various regions. This sector is widespread in the country and is a promising candidate for taking the leadership and managing the PURA complexes in an integrated way. Also major businesses in India with widespread rural services have an experience of maintaining large rural-urban networks. PURA enterprises can undertake management of schools, health care units, vocational training centres, chilling plants, silos and building a market, building of local industrial/ ICT parks, tourism services, banking system and the regional business or industrial units. A new management style has to emerge for managing such type of PURA enterprises. This new PURA enterprise needs partnership from the bank, educational institutions, Government and the private entrepreneurs. The management system should have the flexibility to be competitive and the country has to experiment several models depending on local needs.

Structural Support for PURA

Leading industrial houses should identify the PURA complexes in the areas in their vicinities and adopt them right now, so that they can be developed in an integrated way. They should create a holistic plan of products and services, skills and entrepreneurship. Determination of products and services should be done on the basis of the core strength of the region and the availability of raw materials and infrastructure as well as comparative advantage. Once the product is determined it will also involve infusion of new technologies for making it attractive for both national and international market and also productivity enhancement. After establishing the process and methods a vocational training package needs to be established for improving the skill sets of the local population. Of course some persons may also be brought from other parts of India as it is necessary to have knowledge-skill sharing to increase growth. This is also the time for developing entrepreneurs with leadership qualities who will then create and nurture the enterprise. The selection of entrepreneurs should be preferably done from the higher educational institution in the region, but not necessarily limited to as a rule. This will enable creation of the village level industries simultaneously with the establishment of connectivities in the region.

Each PURA depending upon the region will cost between Rs. 100-200 crores. After initial short term employment during construction etc., we may have to plan for initiating actions for providing regular employment opportunities for 3000 employees. If the industrial / ICT parks are marketed well, they can generate employment opportunities in service and support sector for about

10000 people. This one way of reducing the employment gap leading to upliftment of the 260 million people living below the poverty line and also to provide better jobs for many millions who are technically above poverty line, but poor by many other standards.

In brief, we should generate the business plan for PURA and evolve methodologies for creating a model that would:

- Create a data base of core competencies and comparative advantages in the chosen region.

- Estimate the cost of implementing PURA.

- Measures of quantitatively establishing the economic prosperity of people before and after PURA is implemented.

- Economic returns and self-sustainability.

- Marketing methods for making the PURA self- sustaining and to attract investments.

- Identify key business persons, public persons and others who can manage PURA successfully and also bring in investments.

I am sure many among you can develop such a business plan that will attract business enterprises towards investing in PURA and make PURA a socially relevant and economically feasible enterprise.

Implementation Plan for PURA

The PURA implementation can be effectively done through establishment of an apex body chaired by top management of the nation. The overall PURA scheme will function under this apex body which will provide policy guidelines for promoting PURA in different regions. Five regional PURA corporations may be formed which will execute the PURA in that regions such as North, East, West, South and Central regions with the empowered chairman. Each PURA will have an empowered mission director, deriving powers from the regional corporations. Each PURA can have the following models: solely run by Government, run by joint venture, run by industry, run by financial institution, run by small scale industries, and collaborative venture of all these combinations and also with educational institutions and R&D organisations for providing knowledge connectivity to the farmers, villagers and entrepreneurs. But the key is to have professional and committed management structure with flexibility and powers at the local operating levels.

The funding can come from the government, through the existing budgetary support, provided to ministry of rural development through various schemes, special allotments to the ministry for execution of certain PURAs, NGOs, NRIs, keen to implement the PURA in certain regions, business houses and banking and financial institutions. The execution status of PURA will be reviewed by the regional corporations every six months and by the apex board once in a year. Based on the review midcourse corrections and policy directions will be provided for facilitating smooth execution of individual PURA missions. The mission directors will remain with the PURA till its completion and profitable performance. There could be conferences organized to share the experiences of different PURA being executed in a region.

The prosperity index of the PURA will be governed by contributions to GDP, increase in income level, and reduction in illiteracy, availability of food at affordable prices, availability of electricity, quality water, sanitation facilities and also livable habitat. This will be measured periodically and submitted to the apex body for information and guidance.

Total number of PURAs in the country could be in the range of seven thousand. The mission is a complex activity needing participation of all the citizens of the nation and creative contribution from entrepreneurs, educationists, scientists, technologists, sociologists, industrialists and economists. PURA in action requires a mission mode business like management, operation and people's participation from the levels of the villages. Our study indicates that in southern parts of the country and

Gujarat, private institutions and state governments are executing certain components of PURA such as health care and education. They are also engaged in agro processing sector and employment generation. It is important to note that PURA business plan cannot be universal to be determined at the central level. It has to be customized and located according to region, state, terrain and also structured to meet the needs of the values, culture and aspirations of the local people. The choice of leadership in managing the PURA, participation of the financial institutions and the evolution of market are region specific. It should be run by persons having a high level of integrity and commitment to people of the location. The evolution of PURA project is indeed a challenging task and is the business of progressive entrepreneurs, PURA in action presents the real mission, task, knowledge empowerment, economic connectivity, marketing aspects, empowered management structure with fund and funding methodologies. I am sure the recommendations given in the Atlas of the Sustainability of Food security 2004' will assist the PURA missions.

I wish the food security summit success in all its missions.

Dr. Kalam's Speeches — II

(At His State Visits)

Friends, we should note that human mind is a unique gift. You can enter into Marvels of Universe only if you have curiosity and thinking. I suggest, thinking should become your capital asset, no matter whatever ups and downs you come across in your life.

- Thinking is progress.

- Non-thinking is stagnation to the individual, organization and the country.

- Thinking leads to action.

- Knowledge without action is useless and irrelevant.

- Knowledge with action brings prosperity.

Look at the sky. We are not alone. The whole universe is friendly to us and conspires only to give the best to those who dream and work. Like Nobel Laureate Subrahmanayan Chandrasekhar discovered the black hole through a quest, why most of the stars shine and few die. Today, using Chandrasekhar limit we can calculate how long the sun will shine. Like, Sir C.V. Raman looked at the sea and the sky, and questioned why the sea should be blue? This led to the birth of Raman Effect, he found the blue of the sea was due to the molecular scattering of light and was not a case of reflection of the sky in water as most people imagined. Like, Albert Einstein, armed with the complexity of the universe, asked the question how the universe was born. The famous equation $E=mc^2$ arrived, which can be used for the generation of electricity using nuclear materials and also lead to nuclear weapons. In India during 1960's one important event took place: Prof. Vikram Sarabhai gave a vision for the nation on the space programme. He said India should build her own rocket system, build communication and remote sensing satellites, integrate and launch from Indian space launch centres and put them into the geosynchronous orbit and sun synchronous orbit. Today India can build any type of rocket systems and satellite and launch in a specified orbit.

Indomitable Spirit

Let us study the characteristics of indomitable spirit. It has two components. The first component is that there must be a vision leading to high goals of achievement. I would like to recall a couplet from Thirukkural by the Poet Saint Thiruvalluvar written 2500 years ago.

It means that whatever may be the depth of the river or lake or pond, whatever may be the condition of the water, the lilly flower always comes out and blossoms. Similarly, if there is a definite determination to achieve a goal even if it is impossible to achieve, the man succeeds. Many of us have gone through large programmes and projects. We would have experienced that success is not in sight and there are many hurdles. The same poet reminds us at this point of time through another couplet which means:

We should never be defeated by any problems. We should become master of the situation and defeat the problems. I consider these two Thirukkurals characterize the indomitable spirit.

Bird Story and My Profession

When I think of my school days, I am reminded of an incident which took place when I was studying in 5th class. I had a teacher, Shri Siva Subramaniam Iyer. He was one of the very good teachers in our school. All of us loved to attend his class and hear him. One day, he was teaching about bird's flight. He drew a diagram of a bird on the blackboard depicting the wings, tail, body structure and the head. He explained how the birds create the lift and fly. He also explained to us how they change direction while flying. Nearly 25 minutes he gave the lecture with various information such as lift, drag, how the birds fly in a formation of 10, 20 or 30 etc. At the end of the class, he wanted to know whether we understood how the birds fly. I said I did not understand how the birds fly. When I said this, he asked the other students whether they understood or not. Many students said that they did not understand. Our teacher was a real teacher and very good teacher. He did not get upset by our response.

In view of this, my teacher said that he would take all of us to the sea shore. That evening the whole class was on the sea shore. We enjoyed the roaring sea waves knocking at the rocks in the pleasant evening. Birds were flying with sweet chirping voice. He showed the sea birds in formation in 10 to 20 numbers. We saw the marvellous formation of birds, with a purpose, and we were all amazed. And we were enjoying the formation of the birds. He showed the birds and asked us, what did we observe? We saw the wings being flapped. He asked us to look at the tail portion with the combination of flapping the wing and twisting the tail. We observed closely and found that the birds in that condition flew in the direction they wanted. Then he asked us, where the engine was and how it was powered. Bird is powered by its own life and the motivation what it wants. All these things were explained to us within 15 minutes. We all understood the whole bird dynamics with practical example. How nice it was! Our teacher was a great teacher, he could give us a theoretical lesson coupled with a live demonstration. This is real teaching. I am sure many of the teachers in schools and colleges will follow this example.

For me, it was not merely an understanding of how a bird flies. The bird's flight entered into me and created a feeling on the seashore of Rameswaram. From that evening, I thought that my future study has to be with reference to flight and flight sciences. I am telling this because my teachers teaching and the event that I witnessed later decided my future career. Then one evening after the classes, I asked the teacher, "Sir, please tell me, how to progress further in learning flight sciences." He patiently explained to me that I should complete high school and then I should go to college

                    Pride of the Nation: Dr. A.P.J. Abdul Kalam

that may lead to education of flight. If I do all these I might do something connected with flight sciences. This advice and the bird flying demonstration given by my teacher really gave me a goal and a mission for my life. When I went to college, I took Physics. When I went to engineering in Madras Institute of Technology, I took Aeronautical Engineering.

Thus my life was transformed as a rocket engineer, aerospace engineer and technologist. That one incident of my teacher's teaching, giving a live demonstration, proved to be a turning point in my life which eventually shaped my profession.

Enlightened Citizens

In every country, the national development, which is a collective process, has to be accomplished through the constructive efforts of enlightened citizens, who practise righteousness in all their activities. The evolution of enlightened human beings is indeed a big challenge for the world community. I was asking myself, what will be the components of such a mission? There are three components to that. The first component is education with value system, second religions graduating into spiritual forces to bring universal brotherhood and the third is poverty eradication by attaining economic prosperity through a national vision. And it has to be done in every country in an integrated way with link to the world.

Righteousness

I would like to share a hymn that I heard in the divine campus. The name of the hymn is 'Peace in the World':

Where there is righteousness in the heart

There is a beauty in the character.

When there is beauty in the character,

There is harmony in the home.

When there is harmony in the home,

There is an order in the nation.

When there is order in the nation,

There is peace in the world.

Friends, we can see a beautiful connectivity between heart, character, nation and the world. How to inject righteousness in the human heart? This is indeed the purpose of human creation—that is divinity. We are going through a complex situation as many of us are completely at war with ourselves, with society and with nation. At every instant there is a war in our mind, whether we should go in one direction or another. Whenever there is a dilemma, we must seek the wisdom from the Almighty to lead us to the path of righteousness through education with value system.

Before concluding I would like to administer a 10-point oath to you.

Ten-point Oath for the Youth of the Nation

1. I will pursue my education or the work with dedication and I will excel in it.

2. From now onwards, I will teach at least 10 persons to read and write.

3. I will plant at least 10 saplings and shall ensure their growth through constant care.

4. I will visit rural and urban areas and permanently wean away at least 5 persons from addiction and gambling.

5. I will constantly endeavour to remove the pain of my suffering brethren.

6. I will not support any religious, caste or language differentiation.

7. I will be honest and endeavour to make a corruption- free society.

8. I will work for becoming an enlightened citizen and make my family righteous.

9. I will always be a friend of the mentally and physically challenged and will work hard to make them feel normal, like the rest of us.

     Pride of the Nation: Dr. A.P.J. Abdul Kalam

10. I will proudly celebrate the success of my country and my people.

Conclusion

Through my visits to States, I have gained first-hand knowledge about the aspirations of the people. I am able to interact with common people and know their problems and challenges. I am also able to know about the core competencies of each state and how it can be used for the development of the state itself. Wherever I went the people and students have given me one message that they want to live in a prosperous, peaceful, happy and secure India.

The second important aspect of my visit is to bring the religions graduating to spirituality and promotion of civilisational heritage.

Students should fix a goal in their life, concentrate to combat and overcome the hurdles and achieve excellence. They must imbibe moral values. They should aspire to become entrepreneurs. During holidays students can teach poor and underprivileged children and create a mission for them. They can plant trees and contribute towards improving ecological balance. These activities will collectively lead towards development and prosperity.

I wish you all students and the teaching community success in giving the nation empowered, learned young with integrity.

Speech: Ayodhya as the "Humanity's Healing Center" Sep 20 2010

Ayodhya is a divine land which is enriched with the faith of two religions, both of which have been the cornerstone of human civilization. It represents the cradle of human history and its timeless struggles and triumphs. I was thinking what this holy land, would be known for, in the future India?

I visualize the holy land of Ayodhya to emerge as an unblemished symbol of humanity's quest for service and beacon of the nation's spirit of harmonious integrity by the year 2020. I envisage Ayodhya to be the founding place for a state-of-the-art center of multidimensional healing center and a place which alleviates the pain of all forms – physical, mental and spiritual. It should have four essential features.

First, it should develop as a low-cost healthcare center for all age groups which acts as the home for the best health services especially for the poor and elderly of the nation. It should operate on the patterns already existing in India like those where 70% patients are treated free. It should be a place where hundreds of doctors are dedicated to give vision to a million visually impaired every year, where multi-dimensional experts give mobility to handicapped and give hope to those in abject despair. It should be a center where the Modern medicine finds confluence with the traditional medical systems of ayurveda, yunani, siddha, naturopathy and yoga to heal the body and deliver compassionate healthcare to the needy.

Second, it should emerge as a center of excellence for highest quality research which generates technological solutions to national health problem which afflict the masses. Even as we graduate as the 4th largest economy (PPP) in the world, we still see a time where every second child born in the nation is malnourished and 53 out every 1000 live infants do not live to their first birthday. Similarly, almost half of the worldwide tuberculosis patients are Indians, and anemic levels in Indian women are amongst the highest in the world, exceeding 60% in some states. Availability of clean water and nutritious food still remains to be the foremost enemies in the lives of the millions. Humanity Healing Center should focus on how such stark realities, which are amongst the most prominent national concerns, can be addressed in an effective, pervasive and cost efficient manner especially to reach the remote rural sectors of the nation where 700 million people live. It should be a center which, in collaboration with international agencies, researches low cost preventive vaccine development for diseases which have plagued humanity for ages.

Third, the **"Humanity Healing Center"** would accentuate the amalgamation of the physical healing and spiritual healing. It should emerge a multi-religious spiritual platform, with lush greenery vibrant with colorful life of flowers and birds synchronizes with best healing for soul and treats the spirit. With its proximity to multiple rich religions, the Healing Center would derive the best out of all faiths, and use it as a therapy to treat the ailing souls. It would thus be a place of spiritual learning where humans would find proximity with the divinity and the conscience of the human soul shall awaken.

The fourth pillar of the **Humanity Healing Center** would be based on the foundation of imparting value based knowledge to all from around the world. It would be a crucible for confluence of diverse faith which would facilitate the youth to imbibe and adhere to values which the nation would be proud of. The question is, can the religions converge at Ayodhya, and lead to the creation of society which is healed free from corruption and moral turpitude? Humanity Healing Center would be a place where the best moral education syllabus would be research across the spectrum of multiple religions, and the most efficient methodology to deliver it to the youth be put to practice.

Who will create such a center? I propose the center to be jointly created, owned and operated in the Public Private Community Partnership (PPCP) mode with Government, all parties, organizations, join together with professionals from different fields, retired servicemen and scholars from all communities and all the other stakeholders. The government and private sector may also support the development of the center which would be a symbol of healing to humanity regardless of their color, religion, caste, gender or nationality.

Thus, we see Ayodhya, in another decade to be the world's renowned place for evolution of the enlightened citizenship. A place of healing where value based education is imparted, a place where multiple religions converge along their shared spirituality and where ideas are unbounded by the shackles of the division and where creativity is unleashed for the national transformation. The unity of people is very important, because inimical forces are working against our economic growth, social peace and prosperity, while we are progressing towards knowledge society.

The transformed Ayodhya will have a significant impact on the future of the nation and its one billion people. Today, it stands a defining moment, with consequences which will have far reaching effects. It is our great opportunity today to shape our present action, based on our aspirations of the future rather than let it be governed by the baggage of hostility from the past. Our future generation will revere us for such an action which will help humanity and not the actions which destroy harmony and peace. It is now the golden opportunity of this generation, to be remembered as harbingers of lasting fraternity and enlightened nation rather than generators of thousand year conflicts. This autumn, the resolution to create the Humanity's Healing Center at Ayodhya would be a colossal step to shed the leaves of past, and create a future which all communities and above all, humanity and nation shall cherish and be inspired.

The people of the nation, the Parliament and the State Assembly may discuss and debate this suggestion and how Ayodhya's Humanity's Healing Center may be evolved.

      Pride of the Nation: Dr. A.P.J. Abdul Kalam

Dr. Abdul Kalam's Interview

"Unless India stands up to the world, on one will respect us. In this world, fear has no place. Only strength respects strength"

As a devote Muslim, he prays twice a day. But he is also a Ram bhakt, plays the veena, loves the Shri raga, writes poetry in Tamil and, like every proud Indian, swears by Pokhran II and self-sufficiency in science and technology. Dr. A.P.J. Abdul Kalam is not just another Dr. Strangelove having a torrid affair with the bomb. He is clever, sensitive, amazingly creative and, above all, a soft spoken patriot. India's answer to Western technological arrogance.

What is your vision of India in the new millennium?

I have three visions for India. But before I speak about them I have one question to ask you. Can you tell me why, in 3000 years of our history, people from all over the world have come and invaded us, captured our land, conquered our minds? From Alexander onwards. The Greeks, the Portuguese, the British, the French, the Dutch, all of them came and looted us, took over what was ours. Yet we have not done this to any other nation. We have not invaded anyone. We have not conquered anyone. We have not grabbed their land, their culture, their history and tried to enforce our way of life on them. Why?

Because, I guess, we respected the freedom of others.

Absolutely right. That is why my first vision is that of freedom. I believe that India got its first vision of this in 1857, when we started the war of independence. It is this freedom that we must protect and nurture and build upon. If we are not free, no one will respect us.

My second vision for India is development. For fifty years we have been a developing nation. It is time we saw ourselves as a developed nation. We are among the top five nations of the world in terms of GDP. We have a 10 per cent growth rate in most areas. Our poverty levels are falling. Our achievements are being globally recognized today. Yet we lack the self-confidence to see ourselves as a developed nation, self-reliant and self-assured. Read the last chapter of my book, India 2020, A Vision for the Next Millennium and you will get what I mean.

I have a third vision. That India must stand up to the world. I have written 12 chapters on that. Because I believe that unless India stands up to the world, no one will respect us. In this world, fear has no place. Only strength respects strength. We must be strong not only as a military power but also as an economic power. Both must go hand in hand.

These are visions. What about the reality? What do you see as the most significant achievements of your rather distinguished career culminating in a Bharat Ratna in your lifetime?

My good fortune was to have worked with three great minds. Dr. Vikram Sarabhai of the Department of Space. Professor Satish Dhawan, who succeeded him. And Dr. Brahm Prakash, father of nuclear material. I was lucky to have worked with all three of them closely and consider this the greatest opportunity of my life.

I see four milestones in my career. One: The twenty years I spent in Indian Space Research Organisation. I was given the opportunity to be the project director for India's first satellite launch vehicle, SLV3. The one that launched Rohini. These years played a very important role in my life as a scientist.

Two: After my ISRO years, I joined the Defence Research and Development Organisation and got a chance to be part of India's guided missile programme. It was, you could call, my second bliss when Agni met its mission requirements in 1994.

Three: The department of atomic energy and the DRDO had this tremendous partnership in the recent nuclear tests, on May 11

Pride of the Nation: Dr. A.P.J. Abdul Kalam

and 13. This was my third bliss. The joy of participating with my team in these nuclear tests and proving to the world that India can make it. That we are no longer a developing nation but one among them. It made me feel very proud as an Indian.

And, finally, four: The fact that we have now developed for Agni a re-entry structure, for which we have developed this new material. Avery light material called carbon-carbon. (One day an orthopaedic surgeon from the Nizam Institute of Medical Sciences (in Hyderabad) visited my laboratory. He lifted the material and found it so light that he took me to his hospital and showed me his patients. There were these little girls and boys with heavy metallic calipers weighing over 3 kg each, dragging their feet around. He said to me, "Please remove the pain of my patients." In three weeks, we made these Floor Reaction Orthosis 300 gram calipers and took them to the orthopaedic centre. The children could not believe their eyes! From dragging around a 3 kg load on their legs, they could now move around freely with these 300 gram calipers. They began running around! Their parents had tears in their eyes. That was my fourth bliss.

Apart from science and technology, what else interests you?

Poetry and music. I have got a big library at home and my favourite poets are Milton, Walt Whitman and Ravindranath Tagore. I write poetry too. My book of poems, Yenudaya Prayana, has now been translated into English. It is called My Journey. You must read it. I will send you a copy.

Who are your favourite poets in Tamil, the language you write in?

Bharatidasana, who died in 1965? And Subramaniya Bharathiar, who died in 1939 at the age of 35, killed by an elephant while giving it a coconut. I also enjoy carnatic music and play the veena.

What is your favourite raga?

The Shri raga. You know my favourite kirtan? It is the one that Swami Thyagaraja, a Ram bhakt like me, recited in the Shri raga when he was called by this powerful Tanjore king to sing a poem in his sabha. He sang: "In this gathering whoever are great in front of God, I salute them." He never said: I salute the king. That is strength of conviction. That is courage.

You have asked me so many questions. May I ask you two?

By all means.

Tell me, why is the media here so negative? Why are we in India so embarrassed to recognize our own strengths, our achievements? We are such a great nation. We have so many amazing success stories but we refuse to acknowledge them? Why? We are the second largest producer of wheat in the world. We are the second largest producer of rice. We are the first in milk production. We are number one in remote sensing satellites. Look at Dr. Sudarshan. He has transformed the tribal village into a self-sustaining, self-driving unit. There are millions of such achievements but our media is only obsessed with bad news and failures and disasters.

I was in Tel Aviv once and I was reading this Israeli newspaper. It was the day after a lot of attacks and bombardments and deaths had taken place. The Hamas had struck. But the front page of the newspaper had this picture of a Jewish gentleman who in five years had transformed his desert land into an orchard and a granary. It was this inspiring picture that everyone woke up to. The gory details of killings, bombardments, deaths, were inside the newspaper, buried among other news. In India we only read about death, sickness, terrorism, crime. Why are we so negative?

I guess we grew up with the maxim that good news is no news. The right to publish bad news has become synonymous with freedom. That is why our press is so strong, so fiercely independent—if not always encouraging of success stories.

Another question: Why are we, as a nation, so obsessed with foreign things? Is it a legacy of our colonial years? We want foreign television sets. We want foreign shirts. We want foreign technology. Why this obsession with everything imported? Do we not realize that self-respect comes with self-reliance?

I guess that comes from repression. When you lock your

economy for years and leave it in the hands of local pirates and cheating banias, you are bound to get a backlash. Foreign things have indeed come in but they have also brought down prices, taught us quality, stopped us from cheating consumers with shoddy, overpriced local products. Like in cars, consumer electronics, fabrics, processed foods. Nationalism for too long has been a convenient cover for looting. Let us not forget that. But yes, I agree with you, it is time we started giving value to ourselves as a people, as a nation.

I was in Hyderabad giving this lecture, when a 14- year-old girl came up and asked me for my autograph. I asked her what her goal in life was. She replied: I want to live in a developed India. For her, you and I will have to build this developed India. You must proclaim this through your writings, through your speeches in Parliament.

Dr. Kalam : Quotes

1. You have to dream before your dreams can come true.
2. We will be remembered only if we give to our younger generation a prosperous and safe India, resulting out of economic prosperity coupled with civilizational heritage.
3. Look at the sky. We are not alone. The whole universe is friendly to us and conspires only to give the best to those who dream and work.
4. If a country is to be corruption free and become a nation of beautiful minds, I strongly feel there are three key societal members who can make a difference. They are the father, the mother and the teacher.
5. My message, especially to young people is to have courage to think differently, courage to invent, to travel the unexplored path, courage to discover the impossible and to conquer the problems and succeed. These are great qualities that they must work towards.
6. For great men, religion is a way of making, friends;small people make religion a fighting pool.
7. The country does not deserve anything less than success from us. Let us aim for success.
8. It is very easy to defeat someone but it is very hard to win someone.
9. Be active! Take on responsibility. Work for the things you believe in! If you do not, you are surrendering your fate to others.
10. If you want to leave your footprints on the sands of time, do not drag your feet.
11. Learning gives creativity, creativity leads to thinking, thinking provides knowledge, knowledge makes you great.
12. Suffering is the essence of success!!!
13. If you fail, never give up because FAIL means "First Attempt In Learning".

14. End is not the end, if fact END means "Effort Never Dies" - If you get No as an answer, remember NO means "Next Opportunity". So, let's be positive.

15. Man needs his difficulties because they are necessary to enjoy success.

16. One of the very important characteristics of a student is to question. Let the students ask questions.

17. Dream is not that which you see while sleeping it is something that does not let you sleep.

18. Why be afraid of difficulties, sufferings and problems? When troubles come, try to understand the relevance of your sufferings. Adversity always presents opportunities for introspection.

19. Behind the parents stands the school, and behind the teacher the home.

20. Dream, Dream, Dream. Dream transforms into thoughts, and thoughts result in action.

21. Be more dedicated to making solid achievements than in running after swift but synthetic happiness.

22. Without your involvement you can't succeed. With your involvement you can't fail.

23. Failure will never overtake me if my determination to succeed is strong enough.

24. Once your mind stretches to a new level it never goes back to its original dimension.

25. Don't take rest after your first victory because if you fail in second, more lips are waiting to say that your first victory was just luck.

26. All Birds find shelter during a rain. But Eagle avoids rain by flying above the Clouds.

27. Man needs difficulties in life because they are necessary to enjoy the success.

28. If you want to shine like a sun. First burn like a sun.

29. All of us do not have equal talent. But , all of us have an equal opportunity to develop our talents.

30. Without your involvement you can't succeed. With your involvement you can't fail.

31. You have to dream before your dreams can come true.

32. Thinking is the capital, Enterprise is the way, Hardwork is the solution.

Dr Kalam –A legend Summing up …..

Our Nation has Lost a Real Bharat Ratna.

The Legend - APJ Abdul Kalam :

DR. APJ Abdul Kalam is a God's gift to our nation. He was a great inspiration for all people especially the youth. It's difficult to find such a great and humble person like him. Until his last breath he was with the students, inspiring them with his speech. APJ has made each and every moment in his life worthwhile. The last message delivered by him to the students of IIM-Shillong is " Be courageous to invent something and travel more". He has given us an inspiration "Dream, Dream, Dream. Dreams transform into thoughts And thoughts result in action". His departure is a big loss for the entire nation. It owe a responsibility to "The missile Man", APJ Abdul Kalam, a great Legend .We must fulfill his dreams that he held close to his heart for our nation.

Arrival of Kalam into the World: Avul Pakir Jainulabdeen Abdul Kalam was born on 15th October 1931 in Rameshwaram, Tamilnadu, India to Jainulabudeen and Ashiamma. His father was a ferry owner and was the only source of income for their family. Kalam gave his contribution to his family by disturbuting newspapers.

Education: Abdul Kalam did his schooling in Schwartz Matriculation School, Ramanathapuram and continued his college studies by taking Physics as his core subject in St. Joseph's College, Tiruchirappalli. After completing his graduation in 1954, he went to Madras to study aerospace engineering in Madras Institute of Technology.

Pride of the Nation: Dr. A.P.J. Abdul Kalam

Career: Kalam started his career as scientist in Aeronautical Development Establishment of the Defence Research and Development Organisation and he was also a part of Indian National Committee for Space Research. In July 1980 he was the ISRO project director of India's first Satellite Launch Vehicle (SLV-III) which was deployed Rohini satellite in near-earth orbit. Polar Satellite Launching Vehicle (PSLV) and SLV-III are the projects that were successfully completed by Dr. APJ Abdul Kalam. He played a major part in developing many missiles under the mission including Agni and Prithvi. From 1992 to 1999, Kalam served as the Chief Scientific Adviser to the Prime Minister and the Secretary of the Defence Research and Development Organisation. Along with Rajagopal Chidambaram, he served as a Chief Project Coordinator during the testing phase of Pokhran-II nuclear tests which has made him to be known as the country's best nuclear scientist. He was a visting Professor of Indian Institute of Management in Shillong, Ahmedabad and Indore. He worked as a Professor in Aerospace Engineering at Anna University and Chancellor of the Indian Institute of Space Science and Technology Thiruvananthapuram. With the central theme of defeating corruption Kalam launched "What Can I Give Movement" Programme for the Youth of India.

Kalam as a President: APJ Abdul Kalam was the 11th President of India, first scientist to occupy Rashtrapati Bhawan and was the third President of India to have been honoured with the India's highest civilian honour, Bharat Ratna before becoming the President. People's President has done implemented many reforms when he was the President including signing the "Office of Profit Bill" and supporting the need of "Uniform Civil Code" in India.

Awards: Abdul Kalam has been honoured with many awards and was recognized as a honorable person in other countries also. United Nations has declared his 79th birthday as World Student Day. To celebrate the visit of Kalam to Switzerland in 2005, they have declared 26th May as Science Day. Kalam has received doctorates from 40 universities. To honour his work in ISRO and DRDO and his role as a scientific advisor to the Government, he received the Padma

Bhushan and Padma Vibhushan from the Government of India.

Books: Books of Kalam have kindled several minds and influenced many people. Some of his popular books are India 2020, Wings of fire, Ignited Minds, Mission India, Envisioning an Empowered Nation, Forge your Future and Target 3 Billion.

Kalam's Departure from earth: While delivering his lecture at the Indian Institute of Management Shillong on "The Livable Planet Earth", Kalam fainted at around 6:30 p.m on 27 July 2015. Immediately he was taken to Bethania Hospital in a critical condition and was admitted in the intensive care unit. They confirmed that his death was due to a massive cardiac arrest. He has left us at his 83rd age but he will live in hearts of million people forever. Once he said that "Don't declare holiday on my death, instead work an extra day, if you love me". To obey his words Government of India announced that there will be a seven day state mourning for the tribute of Dr. APJ Abdul Kalam but there will be no holiday. Let's take a pledge to fulfill all his dreams that he had for our nation and youth.